There Were Children in This House

Selected Stories from "Thinking Allowed"

Butch Blume

There Were Children in This House

Copyright 2014 Roy W. Blume, Jr.

ISBN: 978-0-692-33375-4

PRINTED IN THE UNITED STATES OF AMERICA

For Debbie, Katie and Amy:
My guiding constellation

Foreword

It seems only yesterday when a young man entered my office seeking employment. It turned out to be a lucky day for him after I hired him. It also turned out to be a very good decision for The Journal.

That young man was Butch Blume. Through these long years of newspapering, I have met some remarkable people. It was my good fortune to meet him. Without a doubt, he is a talented newsman and one of the best editors I ever had.

It is also my pleasure to call Butch a friend. His family is fortunate to have a husband, father and grandfather with such talent and, I shouldn't fail to mention, a loving heart.

William C. Meade
Williamston, S.C.

Introduction

When I joined the staff of The Journal, a weekly newspaper based in Williamston, South Carolina, I embarked on one of the best experiences I've ever known. I liked everything about the place: the deadlines, the darkroom, the local correspondents, my coworkers, the community, the staccato clacking of typewriters on deadline day, the vaguely sweet smell of printer's ink. The rhythms of a small-town newspaper remaking itself each week appealed to me, and the Journal's steady beat seemed to synchronize with my own pulse.

Of all the things I loved about working at a weekly newspaper, the one thing that has endured and been my traveling companion over the thirty years since I punched the time clock at The Journal is "Thinking Allowed," a personal column that publisher Bill Meade kindly allowed me to write. I mean, what does a twenty-something really have to say, anyway? I wasn't sure, but I knew I wanted to try. Perhaps the fact that I was about to become a father might provide some inspiration. Our first daughter was born, and I wrote about the experience. I saw the column in print, with my byline, and I was hooked. I had found a way to do Facebook two decades before it was invented.

Over the next twenty-five years, I continued to share stories and musings about my wife and kids, my thoughts on space exploration, and my memories of growing up in L.A. (Lower Anderson). It was all very self-indulgent, and I felt an uneasy twinge every time I put something personal out there for others' consumption. (Again, what did I know?) But, every once in a while, I would hear from a total stranger who told me he or she enjoyed reading the column. That was enough to send me back to the typewriter. Bill Meade—and, later, his sons David and Richard—continued to publish the column after I moved on to other jobs, and for that I will always be grateful. I am also thankful to Elaine Ellison-Rider, publisher of The News-Chronicle in Belton, who published "Thinking Allowed" during the years our family lived in that pretty little town.

I didn't write the column without interruption. Sometimes I would take two or three weeks off, and the break would somehow turn into a year or two. I once went five years without writing. I missed the chance to chronicle some big events in our family's life, including both my daughters' weddings. I sorely regret that, because the columns by then had become an unofficial record of our family's journey, and our girls' weddings certainly should have been a part of that. So there are some gaps in this book; I hope they aren't so wide that the reader can't leap across them.

This book is not a complete collection of "Thinking Allowed" columns. I've selected the ones that are mostly about life with my wife and kids. After all, these people were the inspiration for the column in the first place, and they continue to be the most real thing in my life.

So, what do I know, anyway? I know Debbie, Katie and Amy. That will always be enough.

There Were Children
in This House

Space

In my dreams I have voyaged with Captain James T. Kirk to the edge of the universe. I have fought alongside Luke Skywalker on a lunar battlefield and huddled by a cosmic campfire swapping adventure stories with fellow space explorers.

I was seven years old when I sat mesmerized in front of the television as an Atlas rocket launched astronaut John Glenn into American hero-dom. Since then I have been hopelessly lost in space. The Final Frontier is my escape. It is where I go to dream, to be astounded, to be reminded that no man really knows where it all started and where, if ever, it all ends.

A significant space event occurred recently. Pioneer 10, a spacecraft designed to study our solar system, said goodbye to the neighborhood and turned toward the vast nothingness of deep space. Gone. An Associated Press writer with a flair for the poetic described it this way: "Pioneer 10 sped beyond Neptune's orbit for an eternal trip through the Milky Way galaxy."

The thought that humans conceived, built and launched something (like a note in a bottle) that someday may be the only evidence you or I ever existed is worth pondering. A billion or so years from now, in a galaxy far, far away, if another life stumbles upon Pioneer 10, he, she or it will know that we were here. But that probably will not happen, because even though there are more stars and planets out there than we can count, Pioneer 10 will never come any closer than three light years to any known star.

Three light years. If you took all the miles the world's armies have marched, man's traveling machines have driven and his war missiles have flown, and multiplied the total distance by the national debt, you would still come up a couple of light years short. And three years is just a walk to the mailbox when it comes to the size of the universe. The sheer vastness of space is spellbinding. Ever since I was a child, captivated by those black-and-white launch-day images, I have longed to travel into the void and experience what it's like.

But I'm not a child anymore. My dreams of exploring the universe have faded, replaced by more earthbound aspirations—like making a living. I used to believe the solutions to the world's problems could be found out there, in space. As starry-eyed as that vision was, I have found another to rival it—right here on the ground. Today, instead of peering into the heavens, I look forward—very soon—to gazing into my unborn child's eyes. I imagine it is where I will go to dream, to be astounded, to be reminded that no man really knows where it all started and where, if ever, it all ends.

A Private Conversation

On July 16, 1983, at 6:20 AM, my wife nudged me awake and whispered with some urgency, "Honey, I think this is it."

And it was. We got up, made sure everything was packed and ready ... and we waited. The contractions grew stronger. Debbie put to use the breathing exercises she had practiced.

It didn't seem real. We were going to have a baby.

A few minutes past eleven, it was time to go to the hospital. We stepped outside our little apartment into the midsummer swelter, and I immediately regretted that our car had no air conditioning. When we reached the hospital thirty minutes later, Debbie's contractions were two minutes apart. She was admitted just after noon, and I was allowed to join her about an hour later. I stood sentry at her side, one eye on the baby's heart monitor and the other on the screen that told us when another contraction was starting. My brave wife Lamaze-breathed her way through each successive wave. I told her she was doing a great job and promised it would be over soon.

It didn't seem real. We were going to have a baby.

At three o'clock, the alarm on the baby's monitor sounded, and I was pushed aside by a surge of nurses. I stood helplessly against the wall and watched as they strapped an oxygen mask onto my wife's face and turned her from side to side in order to shift the baby's position. Debbie stared at me, eyes wide. After a tense few moments, the baby's heart rate slowed to normal. A nurse patted my wife's hand and told her everything was fine.

Just before four o'clock, her doctor said it was time to deliver. I pulled on green scrubs. A minute later, the whole crew—mother-to-be, husband, doctor, and nurses—moved in a cluster toward the delivery room.

It didn't seem real. We were going to have a baby.

———————————

Your parents are anxious about your arrival.

It makes me sad for them to worry.

They will be happy soon, when they meet you. And they will love you and care for you.

I will miss being here.

In your heart will always remain a quiet knowing of here, like the twinkling of a star in the night sky.

I want them to be happy.

You will be the center of their happiness.

I will miss you.

I am always with you, the twinkling star in your heart.

I love you.

I love you.

———————————

At 4:09 PM, Katherine Elizabeth Blume was born. She is very, very real.

Katie Smiles at Daddy

As a new father, I've spent the first few weeks of my daughter's life trying to get her to smile for me—a real, bona fide smile, not the kind that happens as the byproduct of a burp.

I took Katie for a walk the other night. I enjoyed our first time alone. As we walked along the sidewalk, she kicked the blanket away, already asserting her independence. She was not content to lie in my arms, but insisted on being up by my shoulder, where she could watch the night life go by. And it wasn't enough to see where we had gone; she wanted to see where we were headed.

As I supported her chest with one hand and her bottom with the other, she held her wobbly head up and forward. In the dim street lights, her silhouette resembled that of a turtle stretching its head out of its shell, peering ahead and sniffing the wind before starting a perilous journey across the highway.

We came to the elementary school in our neighborhood. We made our way through the playground to the bleachers that lined what used to be a football field. (Many years before, this had been the town's high school.) Sitting on the cool concrete in the darkness, I held my daughter in my lap so I could see her face. She returned my gaze.

I told she might go to this very school someday. I told her how it reminded me of the school I attended as a boy and about the times I spent on the playground during recess. I told her about the time I kicked a home run in kickball, and I told her about the time during a baseball game when a fly ball hit me right between the eyes. I told her about the time in first grade when a girl named Cathy kissed me and how I slapped her right in the face and how Miss Elrod missed the kiss but saw the slap and boy did I get in trouble.

And I told her about Biff.

"Katie, Biff was big for his age. He started shaving in the fourth grade. When he finally dropped out of school he became a professional wrestler. He was big.

"One day we were playing flag football, which was supposed to be a non-contact sport, only Biff didn't see it that way. He saw it as a chance to run over scrawny squirts like your daddy. I was pretty quick for a squirt, though, and I managed to swipe Biff's red flag on more than one occasion that day. He didn't appreciate that, and I could see he was getting mad.

"When recess was almost over, Biff's team lined up for one last play. The quarterback took the snap and handed it right off to Biff— no fake or anything. Biff grabbed the ball and headed straight up the middle, right at me. I thought I knew what his strategy was. Rather than try to outrun me, he was going to run right at me, then, at the last instant, dart to one side or the other to avoid having his flag stolen by me. I stood my ground, waiting to see which way he would cut. But he didn't cut. He ran right over me, knocking me flat on my back. I had trouble catching my breath.

"I heard the red team cheering and turned to see Biff and the rest of them standing on the other side of the goal line. Then they started laughing at me.

"I wiped my bloody nose with the handkerchief I was holding. Wait. What handkerchief? It was Biff's flag! I jumped up and waved it for everybody to see. Then the bell rang, and recess was over. I walked up to Biff, smiled, and tossed him his flag. I didn't say anything. He was big, you know.

"So what do you think about that, Katiebug?"

She gazed at me and realized I wasn't making noises with my mouth anymore. Then she smiled.

My little girl smiled at me.

Thanks, Biff.

I'm Safe

On the day when you stand in front of your family and friends and promise to love, honor and cherish, not once does the minister say anything about how you are supposed to deal with your beloved's unconventionalities.

We all have things about us that are weird—unusual habits we suppress in public, feelings we reveal only to our closest friends. We're all a little strange, but we're okay with our own oddities. It's another adventure altogether when you marry someone and take on a whole new world of weirdness.

Take my wife. Her thing is to feel "safe." Just how does one communicate the sensation of feeling safe? Well, the word "safe," preferably squealed with childlike glee, is the best way to describe it.

Maybe a few real-life examples will help. When Debbie was a little girl, she, her sister and their parents would take vacation trips in the family station wagon. Just when things started to get dull, Debbie, overcome by her urge to feel safe, would crawl to the rear of the car, pull the suitcases up around her in a kind of fort, and taunt her younger sister: "Look, Beth! I'm safe and you're not!" Beth would wail, and Daddy would have to stop the car and build a wall of suitcases for Beth so that she could be safe, too.

There also were times when Debbie and Beth would pull out an old quilt while their mom was at work—Ida Ruth, the babysitter, let them get away with far too much—and drape it across the clothesline and "play tent." "Mama would kill us when she came home," Debbie said, "but we felt safe for the moment." She also felt safe on Saturday afternoons when her mom let them set up their card table outside by the sandbox and eat supper.

This delightful trait of hers, being safe, has carried over into adulthood. Whenever there's a storm brewing, Debbie scurries to the couch and barricades herself in the corner by piling the pillows around her. In such moments of supreme safeness, she enjoys squealing, "I'm so safe I could scream!" And she actually does scream. She has told me there is almost no safer feeling in the world than to be wrapped up in a quilt, lying on the couch and watching a football game while a steady rain beats against the roof.

When I asked her if I could write a public column about her need to feel safe, she said she was afraid people would think she was crazy. Okay, time for a little self-disclosure: I understand Debbie. As a boy, I felt safe inside my imaginary space capsule in my closet or when I was high up in a tree where I could see everybody but nobody could see me. I felt safe in the porch swing at my Papa's house. Today, when I remember those places, I feel safe all over again.

We build walls and roofs to keep us safe from the elements. We build savings accounts to keep us safe from financial ruin. We seek eternal safety through religion. We all want to feel safe. And no wonder. Another Marine was killed in Beirut yesterday. A thirty-four-year-old mother died in Piedmont when she pulled her car in front of a truck she never saw. Two Pickens people pleaded guilty this week to kidnapping, robbing and raping their next-door neighbor.

The world is not always a safe place, so we seek islands of safety. My daughter, Katie, only three months old, already knows what being safe feels like. You can see it when her mother feeds her or when her daddy puts her to his shoulder and sings her off to sleep.

When you stand in front of the minister and promise to love, honor and cherish, he ought to add a little something about making sure she feels safe every day.

There is one thing that Debbie says makes her feel safer than anything else in the world, and that's when I hold her. How crazy is that?

Dear Mr. Claus

Dear Mr. Claus:

My name is Katherine Elizabeth Blume. You can call me Katie. In fact, you can call me Katiebug, even though I am not a bug—that's just what my mommy and daddy call me.

I'll call you Santa, if that's okay.

I got my middle name from my Aunt Beth, who used to tell people her name was Miss Elizabeth Beth Ann Davenport. When she was a kid, she never believed people when they told her that "Elizabeth" and "Beth" are the same name. She's grown up and married now, and her name is Mrs. Shawn Reid Elizabeth Beth Ann Davenport McGee.

Mommy and Daddy decided to name me Katherine because they thought it sounded distinguished. I was only a few hours old, but I remember when they decided on the name. Daddy said it over and over, as though it made him feel warm inside: "Katherine ... Katherine ... yes, I like the sound of that ... Katherine."

You know what, Santa? I don't think my daddy has ever called me Katherine since. I think he said it so many times the first day that he used it all up. Now he just calls me Katiebug.

Let me get to the point. I've been told by reliable sources that every Christmas Eve you fly all around the world on a sleigh pulled by eight reindeer, bringing presents to all the good little boys and girls. Is this true, and do I qualify? I'm only five months old, but I haven't done anything really bad. Sometimes Daddy covers his head with a pillow when I wake up crying in the middle of the night, and sometimes I spit up on Mommy's couch. Please talk to my Nanny Davenport. She says I'm good as gold. I can provide other references upon request.

I've also heard that you come down the chimney when you bring the presents. Again, I have to ask: Do I qualify? We don't have a chimney. If you would consider coming to the front door, I'm sure my parents would let you in. Mommy could give you some of her homemade soup and cornbread, and you could watch TV.

I haven't mentioned what I would like for Christmas, but as long as it's something I can hold in my hand or gnaw on, I'll be happy.

In case you are still having a hard time deciding whether or not I qualify for Christmas, let me mention one more thing: Did you know that Katherine means "pure one"?

By the way, is Santa your real name? My Aunt Beth says your real name is Mr. Jolly Old Saint Nicholas Nick Kris Kringle Claus.

Love,
Katherine Elizabeth Katiebug Blume

Moving Experience

I sat on the floor in the kitchen of our empty little apartment. A few hours earlier, the place had seemed smaller, crowded with packing boxes, beds, books and the thousand toys of a six-month-old child.

The apartment was our home for eight months. But on this day we were moving to a house, leaving behind a place where visitors felt comfortable enough to prop their feet up on the coffee table and take a nap.

I thought about what I would remember about the place. This is a ritual I go through when I move—the paying of last respects. I had reserved the moment for myself, waiting until everyone was gone so

I could steal the last goodbye.

I had already checked the other rooms for the final time. Upstairs, when I leaned through the doorway of the bathroom, I saw my reflection in the mirror and smiled, remembering the times I stood on tiptoe in order to shave while my wife leaned over the counter to dry her hair. The new place would have two sinks and a big mirror, but I would miss those close encounters of the early-morning kind.

I walked into our daughter's nursery, and the bare walls reminded me of how empty the room had seemed before Katie came along. We assembled her crib here. After she was born, it was a space that could always warm me on a cold day.

I looked into our bedroom and recalled the only night I'd spent there alone, when Debbie was at the hospital with our newborn child. That was a happy but lonely night for me.

I went downstairs to the living room, a friendly space with a cushiony couch for napping during ball games and a piano so I could lie on the carpet and listen to my wife play her beautiful music.

Finally, the kitchen, the heart of our home, a warm and welcoming room. Sitting in the middle of the floor, it was hard to leave the place behind.

I stood up, dusted myself off and looked around the little apartment for the last time. I'd never made any pictures of the place. Our daughter's first home, but no photos with which to remember it.

I left the keys on the counter, stepped outside and closed the door.

Goodbye, home. Hello, home.

Trailblazer

My daughter is seven months old, and already she's thinking about what she wants to be when she grows up. As near as I can figure, she's torn between a career in stock car racing or being a stuntwoman on "That's Incredible." It is also possible she wants to be a trash collector.

It started a few months ago when her mother decided she wanted to purchase an inflatable walker.

"She doesn't need one of those things," I protested over the top of my newspaper. "The tubes will make her look like the Michelin Man on roller skates."

She smiled, not lifting her eyes from her needlework.

"Besides," I pleaded, "what's the big hurry with learning to walk? She's perfectly content for me to carry her wherever she wants to go."

Eyeballing me over the top of her glasses, she asked, "Honey, do you plan to carry her down the aisle at her wedding?" She went back to her cross-stitch and let that sink in.

"She's never getting married," I finally said with every bit of authority I could muster. "In fact," I said, turning the page of my newspaper with an air of finality, "she's going to stay with us forever."

"Anything you say, honey."

When I came home from work the next day, the inflatable walker was in my home. Katie must have hit the floor with both feet spinning because, in no time, she was the master of her own universe. It didn't take her long to learn a few tricks, including:

1) Human Bowling Ball. The child has discovered that if she gets

a running start at one end of the hallway, she can gain enough momentum to bowl over the table by the bathroom door and slam her face into the wall at the other end of the hall. Any dreams of our daughter winning the Miss America pageant are fast fading.

2) Human Torch. Like other families trying to save money, we recently purchased a portable kerosene heater. This dangerous piece of equipment is hands-off when it comes to children who don't immediately comprehend the difference between fire and Kool-Aid. Restraints are reinforced with a crisply enunciated "No!" followed by an equally crisp stinger across the back of the offending hand.

This system should work. It does not. My child is smart enough to know the meaning of the word no, but she is also smart enough to think that if she pretends she does not know the meaning of the word, she might get away with no consequences. Also, if she makes her offenses look like accidents, her parents might not scold her. After doing something that's forbidden, she will back herself into the corner of the den and sit there babbling, saying such adorable things as "da-da" and "bye-bye" and making cute noises that we applaud now but will later forbid when she is three and making them while drinking a cup of milk at the dinner table in front of company. When she is convinced we have forgotten her crime, she peels rubber toward the kitchen.

The (unlit) kerosene heater rests along her route to the kitchen. Gathering speed, she zips past and, without slowing or looking, manages to hook its grill with a trailing finger and pop it open. Pretending to be unaware of this "accident," she proceeds to the kitchen to rummage through the trash can.

3) Trash Collector. I know my daughter would not appreciate others knowing she rummages through trash cans, but I choose to reveal it for her own good and in the hope that other parents will feel emboldened to admit that their child would just as soon lick the lining of a Hefty trash bag as a Popsicle.

At least once every hour, Katie makes a pilgrimage to the kitchen trash can, which she tilts in her favor and, enraptured, explores its deepest mysteries. She is very quiet. Hiding, we watch. After a few moments of intense exploration, she lets loose with a primal yelp and jerks the trash bag clear of the can, dragging it and its trailing contents through the rest of the house, jabbering all the way.

I could worry about her face-planting the wall or burning her fingers or gumming a day-old banana peel. Instead, I'll do my best to protect her while also being thankful—if not a little proud—that she has the moxie to get into such mischief.

Don't Walk Too Fast

A few nights ago I was in our little girl's room, trying to coax her to sleep with a few rusty bars of "Amazing Grace." Our ugly but comfortable drab green rocker creaked along in perfect time.

Katie was tired and surrendered easily to bedtime. It had been another busy day. When you're thirteen months old, every day is a new opportunity to explore strange new worlds, to seek out new life and new civilizations living under the couch, and to boldly go where no toddler has gone before—specifically, behind the commode.

She raised her head from its resting place on my chest, rubbed her eyes and yawned. I took the opportunity to count her teeth. My smile was met by hers. "Four toothies!" I whispered, stroking her forehead. She plopped her head back on my chest and, moments later, was snoring lightly.

In the quiet, with her breathing and the squeaky rocker the only sounds in our world, I thought of how she was zipping through childhood. I couldn't believe it when she'd started walking the week before. One day she was crawling after me as I left the room, and when I turned to pick her up she was standing under her own power, concentrating, straining to plant one wobbling leg in front of the other. Within a couple of days she was moving about with the grace of a veteran walker. The familiar "phlapt phlapt" of her feet meeting the floor became another of the child's trademarks, along with her "Spanky face."

As proud as I was, I also knew it meant she would never crawl again. It meant she was a little less dependent on her father and growing less so every day.

I thought of the first time I saw her, the moment she made her entrance into a bright world. A squirming little red creature, she was a gazer from the beginning. Her eyes drank in her surroundings. Even in those initial moments of life outside the safety of her mother's womb, she showed us she was made of inquisitive stuff.

A dog barked, and my thoughts snapped back to the

here-and-now. Time for bed.

I pulled myself out of the comfortable old chair and put my child to bed. She curled her legs under her, turned her head to the side, sighed, and was asleep again, lost in a dream where the world is new every day. I lingered for a moment, then tiptoed away.

Goodnight, Katiebug. Don't walk too fast.

Night and Day

Ever wonder why some people are day people, while others are creatures of the night? Take my parents. If they are visiting about the time the sun is setting, my dad will say, "It's getting dark. Better be getting on home." It doesn't matter where he is or what he is doing; if it's getting dark, it's time to start getting on home.

Sometimes I say to him, "Dad, do you see those glass bowls on the front of your car? Those are called headlights. They literally illuminate the road in front of you so that you can drive at night."

"I know that," my father replies, although I know he is skeptical.

I shouldn't pick on Dad. My wife is also a day person. If she happens to make it past nine-thirty at night without falling asleep on the couch, I'm on the phone inviting the neighbors over to bear witness.

See? I told you she was still awake!

I never would have believed it!

She once stayed up past ten o'clock on Christmas Eve, but that doesn't count.

There must be something tranquilizing about lying on a sofa while the television is blaring and a babbling toddler is coloring the floor. It gives Debbie the nods every time.

When it is a respectably late-enough hour to retire (around midnight for yours truly), it falls upon me to awaken this sleeping beauty. It is no easy thing. After a few minutes of patting and tugging and cajoling on my part (one never uses harsh tactics to awaken this person), she half-opens one eye, looks me straight in the face and says, "Mphglah," and then slides back into unconsciousness.

It is normally about this time that our daughter wakes up and starts to cry. Like her father, she is a night person and cannot stand the thought that everybody else is not awake, too.

There are drawbacks to being a night person in this day-person world of ours, like when the alarm clock goes off at 6:00 AM and my bewildered brain instructs my hand to stuff the clock up my nose. This must be the same kind of neural malfunction that causes my wife to say things like "Mphglah."

It's probably just as well that she is day and I am night. Picture the calamity that would ensue if we both attempted to wake up at the same time.

Cleaver Fever

As I drive around, I see more and more of those big satellite dishes, the ones that look like they could pull in a decent TV signal from the Andromeda Galaxy. People put them anywhere: backyard, front yard, in the garden, behind the outhouse. What possesses someone to plant a giant wok next to a junked '63 Chrysler?

I think I've discovered the answer: It has to be Leave-It-to-Beaver fever. The more channels you can get, the more times a day you can watch Wally and the Beav do some really dopey things.

We don't have a satellite dish, but we have cable TV, which means my wife and daughter can watch Leave It to Beaver at least twice each day. And they do. That fact in itself doesn't bother me. What does is that every now and then my wife gets it in her head that our family should aspire to the lifestyle of Ward and June and the boys.

"I wish we were more like the Cleavers," she is prone to say during one of these spells, "and always eat in the dining room and wear dress-up clothes and say, 'May I please be excused?' And I think it's wonderful how Ward and June always call each other 'dear,'" she says. (Note: My wife insists that I not address her by her given name. It took three years of hard practice to learn to start my sentences with "Honey" instead of "Debbie.")

After she has gone through a list of reasons why we should want to be more like this TV family, I feel compelled to explain to her just why, when it comes to imitating life as Cleavers, the Blume family falls short of the mark.

"Think about it, Deb ... I mean honey. First of all, we are the parents of a daughter who habitually walks up to total strangers and announces: 'That's a hiney!'"

"But she's young. She can be molded in my image," she replies.

"Fine, but what about me? I'm not the Ward Cleaver type. I don't see me wearing a necktie while sitting in my boxer shorts watching the Braves."

"Bad habits should be broken," she says.

"Okay. I didn't want to bring this up, but you've forced me. What about our refrigerator?"

"What about our refrigerator?"

"Yesterday I reached past the green spaghetti, looking for the pimento cheese. Something growled at me."

"Are you insinuating that my refrigerator is not as clean as June Cleaver's?"

"Not saying that. It's just that the last time we cleaned out the fridge and dumped the remains by the woods, a stray dog took a sniff and collapsed on the spot."

That usually brings her to her senses.

"I guess you're right," she says. "We just don't have the right stuff to be Cleavers."

"I agree," I say. "Besides, do we really want our children associating with characters with names like Lumpy, Whitey and Eddie Mundello?"

Terrific Twos

My daughter turned two years old this week, which is quite an accomplishment for someone her age. I consulted our Better Homes and Gardens Baby Book to see what kinds of things my two-year-old should be able to do.

According to the book, an "average, normal child" between the ages of two and three learns to do things like tell first and last names, copy a circle with a crayon, follow simple directions, and be toilet-trained during the day and remain dry all night some of the time. Mind you, that's an "average, normal child." Have you ever met anyone who was the parent of an "average, normal child"?

I've decided to write the folks at Better Homes and Gardens and tell them what it's really like to be a parent of a two-year-old. Here are some of my daughter's noteworthy achievements:

• Mr. Potty—We have finally convinced Katie that Mr. Potty is her friend. The only problem now is that she wants to visit her friend every three-and-a-half minutes.

• Brushy Toothy—Before the child will open her mouth so that I can insert a toothbrush, I have to convince her beyond any rea-sonable doubt that there are wild animals running loose between her teeth and over her tongue and that I alone am qualified to brush them away. Even then she would just as soon let the giraffes camp out amongst her molars.

• Prayer Time—She has taken the prayers we taught her and created her own Reader's Digest condensed versions:

"Now I lay me down to sleep, I pray the Lord amen that's all."

And ...

"God is great, God is good. Let us thank him amen that's all."

• Point and Tell—The child likes to point to parts of other

people's bodies and make pronouncements about them. "That's a nostril" and "That's a hiney" are two of her favorite utterances.

• Ballet—Katie is into ballet. Her favorite pose is achieved by dropping to all fours and sticking one leg up in the air.

• Mr. Doc—Even before her mother turns the station wagon into the parking lot at the doctor's office, the child has already attempted to barter away her pacifier, her Cabbage Patch Preemie and her future earnings for the chance to escape another checkup.

• Let's Sing—My daughter's favorite thing to do is sing. Her favorite song concerns a turtle named Tiny Tim who goes swimming in the bathtub, drinks up all the water, eats up all the soap, and ends up in the hospital with a bubble in his throat (urp). At the end, she gets to imitate the sound of a turtle burping, which, of course, she belches forth with gusto.

These are the kinds of things they don't tell you about in Better Homes and Gardens. The book does say, however, that your child is a baby no more. They tell you that your child will advance by leaps and bounds over the next four years and someday you will suddenly ask yourself where the baby went.

Pretty perceptive for a bunch of gardeners.

Fatherhood

My two-year-old daughter, the botanist, stoops to inspect a lonely dandelion. She manages to ignore a blistering summer sun and a persevering fly that has chosen the runway of her forehead to practice touch-and-goes.

Sagging elegantly in my aluminum lawn chair, I attempt to ignore the heat, but I cannot. It works on me, and my mind wanders. I lock my eyes on my child in a kind of auto-pilot babysitting mode and allow my thoughts to depart this particular time and place ...

"Use both hands!"

Instinctively, the boy moves his right hand to support his left, upon which is perched an oversized baseball glove. Circling under a high pop fly, the boy exults in his father's shouts of encouragement.

Like a satellite failing to achieve orbit, the ball is arrested in its upward flight and now is hurtling earthward. The boy plants himself under the ball, which now moves neither left nor right—only straight down—and prays he will catch it. All too suddenly the ball slams into the oiled leather pocket with a smack—the sound of success. Knocked off balance by the impact but refusing to acknowledge the million bee stings in his palm, the boy grins at the man.

"Good catch, son," the man says.

"Use both hands!" I shout as she determines to climb the back porch steps.

Her independence won't allow her to acknowledge that she has heard and understood, but her hands move to the brick steps, and she steadies herself. The botanist is now a mountain climber.

"Be careful," the man warns as the boy inches toward the edge of the ravine. Far below—perhaps twenty feet—is a pool of water. With fish in it. Fish he intends to catch.

Pressing the release on his Zebco fishing reel, he watches the red and white float drop to the still water below. For long and silent stretches he stares at the motionless float, waiting for it to slip beneath the dark surface. A fussy blue jay squawks. It is five seconds before the boy comprehends that the float has disappeared. He jerks the rod skyward, and everything—float, sinker, hook and fish—spews upward like a surface-to-air missile. In mid-launch, fish and hook part ways. The fish drops at the boy's feet, flops twice, and falls back toward the safety of the water below.

The boy turns to face the man.

"Good try, son," says the man, smiling.

"Be careful!" I yell toward my daughter, who has reached the peak of her Everest and stands proudly atop the conquered. The child looks at me and smiles. I smile back.

I hope I, too, will be a good dad.

Dear Santa

Dear Santa,

It's me again—Katiebug. Things have really changed a lot since my last letter. I am now two and a half years old, and I don't spit up on Mommy's couch anymore. And guess what? The house we live in now has a chimney! I'll make sure my daddy doesn't build a fire on Christmas Eve.

Enough small talk. Let's get to the important stuff, like my

Christmas list. I'm beyond baby toys. At the top of my list this year is a toy kitchen. After all, I should start taking on some responsibilities around the house. I also would like a doctor's kit, a Barbie doll, a Wuzzle (Elaroo is my favorite), a Cabbage Patch electric toothbrush, some books and lots of surprises.

But the one thing I want more than anything is a new baby sister or brother. I don't know if you're in charge of this, but I thought it wouldn't hurt to ask.

I've been a good girl. I've been eating most of my vegetables, I helped Mommy fold the clothes, and I say my prayers every night. If you come to my house on Christmas Eve, you can eat some of my mommy's homemade soup and cornbread.

I hope all this will help you remember who I am. But just in case you don't ... do you know the little kid who stands back and watches while all the other children climb onto your lap and tell you what they want for Christmas? That's me. I'm too shy to talk to you in person, but please know that I think you are wonderful. Maybe next year I'll sit on your lap, but for now I'll just wave and blow you a kiss, if that's okay.

Love,
Katherine Elizabeth Katiebug Blume

Night Moves

"Daddy!"

I look at the alarm clock. It is three o'clock in the morning.

"Daddy!"

It is three o'clock in the morning, and my daughter is not calling for her mother. She is calling for me.

"Daddy!"

Her mother stirs but then is still. I slide from under the warm covers. I negotiate the familiar steps to my daughter's room. I know the path well.

By the faint glow of her nightlight, I can see her sitting up in bed, her hands stretched toward me. "Daddy, I'm scared."

I gather her in my arms and put her in our bed. She burrows into a safe nest between her mother and me and is snoring happily within a minute.

I, on the other hand, am wide awake and will be so for at least another thirty minutes. As my child rolls over and jams her big toe into my right ear, I stare at the ceiling and think. What else does one do at three in the morning?

There were times when my mom or dad had to come to my room to answer my cries in the middle of the night. I felt the need to tell them exactly what was scaring me to death. One night I described the disembodied hand that was crawling across my chest. I knew it still had to be in the room even though I'd swatted at it. I must have been convincing because my mother turned on the light and checked under the bed.

Then there was the time Bloody Bones was hiding under the bed, waiting to grab me every time I closed my eyes. My mother swept under the bed with her broom to prove there was no Bloody Bones hiding there. I said she must know that Bloody Bones can make himself invisible, and she said I could get in her bed because she had to get up and go to work in the morning.

And there were the nightmares of snakes and tornadoes. My parents were right there to hear about my bad dreams and drive the boogers away.

My daughter is just now reaching the age when she can describe her fears to me. I hope I will be patient. A toe in the ear is a small price to pay for a child's peace of mind.

Daddy's Bottle of Time

If I could save time in a bottle,
If words could make wishes come true,
I'd save every day like a treasure, and then,
Again, I would spend them with you. (Jim Croce)

Within the past two weeks we have experienced a major event: the birth of our second child, Amy Elise.

The arrival of a child is a moment we wish we could squeeze into a bottle, to be emptied out and relived whenever we needed it. Such special events are not hard to remember. They so clearly mark our personal history that we could not forget them if we tried. Yet I often find myself removing the top from my bottle of time and pulling out memories of occurrences that are far less important than the birth of a child, less noteworthy than graduating from college.

I sometimes use this space to share some of the ordinary contents of my bottle of time. Memories of childhood, laden with the adventures of a young boy, warm me. The things I remember most clearly are not big events but such everyday occurrences as going fishing with my dad and playing baseball with my brother. They are moments I long ago began squeezing into my bottle of time.

I have not forgotten the day Debbie and I got married. But long after the details of that momentous day have dimmed, I will still be able to reach into my bottle and pull out the memory of the time Debbie and I enjoyed the best hamburger we'd ever tasted at a hotel restaurant 250 miles from home. I will also not forget the day she tried to doctor my sinuses with some industrial-strength homemade saline solution. These times, too, I keep in my bottle.

The birth of our first child, Katie, was one of the most emotionally raw experiences of my life. Yet when I think of my firstborn, it is not that day in the hospital I recall. Rather, I remember a summer night in a neighborhood schoolyard when she looked into my eyes and gave me the gift of her first smile. And while I remember the first time I ever held her in my arms, even stronger is the warmth I feel each night when she wraps her arms around my neck as I read to her the story of Farmer Jones. It's a memory to be squeezed into my crowded little bottle of time.

And now there's Amy, a new person with memories yet to be made. Although she is only two weeks old, I can tell by looking into her eyes that she is not another Katie. She is a different person altogether. I know she will fashion for me some special moments for my bottle.

Welcome, Amy. Already you've given us the memory of your grand entrance into our lives. I look forward to your first word, your first step, your first prom night.

But, most of all, I look forward to sharing with you the everyday moments in your life that will make you distinctly Amy. And when you experience those times, don't be surprised when your daddy is right behind you, opening his bottle of time to see if there's room for one more memory.

The Daughter's Farmer

There is no Farmer Jones at our house tonight.

My daughter Katie and I have a ritual we observe at bedtime. After we brush her teeth, wash her face and put on her PJs, we pull out two books to read. The one about Farmer Jones and his animals always gets picked. The words are simple, and they are memorized:

It is suppertime on the farm.

The animals are very hungry.

But where is Farmer Jones?

It's that last line that makes it all worthwhile for Katie. "But where is Farmer Jones?" she asks, turning up her palms in dramatic bewilderment.

Each page describes a different hungry farm animal asking the same burning question: "But where is Farmer Jones?" This line is reserved for Katie, and any attempt to deny her the joy of repeating it will be met with a swift reprisal.

There aren't too many nights when I don't get to read to her the story of Farmer Jones and his hungry animals. It's a moment at day's end I've come to look forward to. But there will be no story tonight. Katie has decided to spend the night with her grandparents. Our house seems too quiet. It is the first time I have slept under this roof when she wasn't in her own bed just down the hall.

This is only the beginning, my wife tells me, while she rocks our new daughter, Amy, to sleep. "It seems like yesterday we were packing Katie's diaper bag. Before we know it we'll help her pack her bags for college."

Tonight, her grandparents. This spring, perhaps her friends from church. In a few years, maybe summer camp. Before I know where the time has gone, she will be leaving to start her own life and family. How many times have I considered it nothing more than a cliché when people say that children grow up too fast? Now I find myself thinking how true it is.

I hear Debbie lock the back door. I will check it again. I always do. Then I'll check the front door, then the lights, then the thermostat. I follow the same ritual every night.

Then I'll stop by Amy's room and fill her humidifier. Then I'll go to Katie's room, even though she is sleeping somewhere else tonight. I'll touch her pillow, as though to stroke her hair.

Then I'll kiss my wife and try to go to sleep.

But where is Farmer Jones?

Pete and Re-Pete

I would never want to be president of the United States, who has more than enough trouble dealing with a Panamanian dictator and assorted uprisings in Arab states. I couldn't be the president because I can't even control the battles that rage in the back seat of our car.

Two warring factions who shall be identified only as Pete and Re-Pete live back there and say derogatory things about each other. The strategy seems straightforward: to say something so random that one's opponent is pushed beyond the capacity to respond civilly and begins screaming at the top of one's lungs.

What follows is a reconstruction of one such recent throw-down:

Pete (tauntingly): "I have three books."

Re-Pete (bristling): "I have three books."

"No, you have just one book."

"I have three books."

"No, you don't!"

"Yes, I do!"

"No, you don't!" (Accompanied by vigorous head-shaking.)

"Un-HUH!" (Nodding up and down with joy.)

"No, you DON'T! Mommy, tell her she does NOT have three books. Only I have three books!"

Mother: "You'd both better stop screaming right this second or Daddy will pull the car over to the side of the road and feed you both to a herd of turtles."

This brings the screaming match to an abrupt halt. Not because they are afraid of child-eating turtles. Quite the contrary—they beg me to stop the car so they can see for themselves these interesting creatures.

An impartial judge might rule that Re-Pete had won the argument on style points, even though she did not, in fact, have three books. The truth is irrelevant. The whole point of the argument is lost in the heat of the battle.

Pete would protest that Re-Pete had not observed the rules of fair play. Specifically, she had violated the rule that says you cannot say something that is untrue. Re-Pete's assertion that she had three books didn't necessarily make it true, no matter how earnestly she stated it. But that didn't matter to Re-Pete; when you're only two, you can always claim ignorance of the rules. She has learned that style trumps substance in the hardscrabble world of backseat warfare.

Another of the rules of fair play is that neither party is allowed to say something that makes no sense. When you're four and well spoken, you can appreciate that rule's basic fairness. But if you're only two, you can again play dumb, which Re-Pete does, igniting in her older sister an exquisite white rage:

"Stop looking at me!"

"Szcholorbzk!"

"What?"

"Szcholorbzk!"

"WHAT?"

"Szcholorbzk!"

"But that doesn't mean anything!"

"Szcholorbzk!"

"THAT DOES NOT MEAN ANYTHING!"

"Szcholorbzk!"

"Daddy, she said 'szcholorbzk,' and that does not MEAN anything!"

Daddy: "Honey, what does 'szcholorbzk' mean?"

Re-Pete: "Eggoshlraky."

"Thank you, sweetie."

Come to think of it, if I can mediate these backseat hostilities and still keep my family together, maybe I am just the man for the White House. Just give me a couple of seasoned negotiators like Pete and Re-Pete and a hearty herd of fighting turtles, and we'll show Mr. Gorbachev what real diplomacy is.

Home Is Where You Hang Your Pictures

We have purchased our first home.

Had it not been for my wife's encouragement (i.e., hinting,

asking, pleading and threat of divorce) we might still be living in the nice rental house that was the first home for our two children and Clyde, the hamster.

"Why?" I protested, clutching the checkbook. "Why would we want to pay three times as much money every month just to own our own home?"

"Because I want to put a nail in a wall whenever I feel like it," she said, staring at me and calmly slapping the palm of her hand with a claw hammer, which I interpreted as a hostile gesture.

Convinced, I asked for two concessions: a garage and two bathrooms. We reached a settlement quickly on the bathrooms, but you can come by sometime and I'll show you where I plan to add on a garage in the year 2033. On that spot today stands my useful, easy-to-assemble aluminum utility building. I bought it unassembled in order to save money to pay for my new house. Besides, putting together an aluminum building shouldn't be any problem for a guy who can sometimes program his VCR. (I inherited from my father a genetic predisposition for unwarranted self-confidence.)

I suspected things weren't going to be quite as simple as I'd hoped when the directions instructed me to "set aside at least two full days for assembly of your useful, easy-to-assemble utility building." The directions also promised that I could put the whole thing together by myself. That was a lie. Just ask my friend, Eddie. He was there; he saw it—a great metallic sail-like thing, warping and bowing in the gales of a summer thunderstorm, spitting to the heavens the hundreds of screws we had fastened by the sweat of our brows with our nifty cordless screwdrivers. By the time the two of us neared completion of this one-man project, we had driven enough screws to know them by their proper names. ("Could you pass me a D-11 alloy short-tapered flat head, please?")

I can live with an aluminum storage building, but there was no compromise when it came to the subject of bathrooms. Simply put, there would be not less than two. Period. No discussion. We've always lived in a house with only one bathroom. Three women and me. Take a moment to picture it. I am convinced that my five-year-old has been endowed with an extrasensory nervous system that is triggered whenever Daddy goes into the bathroom and shuts the door. BRRAANNNGGG! (Bells, whistles, sirens.) DADDY'S IN THERE! GO TO THE DOOR AND WAIL AS THOUGH YOU ARE DYING! TELL HIM YOU NEED TO GO! NOW! SCREAM UNTIL HE LETS YOU IN! THREATEN IMPENDING BODILY FUNCTION UNTIL HE BELIEVES YOU!

Katie's alarm doesn't go off as often as it used to, but her younger sister is starting to pick up the slack. What's more disconcerting is the fact that even though we now are a two-bathroom family, all four of us still seem to end up in one—shaving, putting on makeup and generally screaming and kicking and gouging. I've experimented with sneaking to the unoccupied bathroom, but within just a few minutes, inexplicably, we are all drawn together again. We are a family unit.

But it's home, and it's ours—a place where we can drive a nail into one of our brand new walls whenever we feel like it, which I started to do the other day when my wife walked into the room.

"Step away from the hammer," she said. "Now."

No Boogers Out Tonight

Katie, our five-year-old, can think of any number of excuses to stay up past bedtime, but when all else fails, she resorts to the tried-and-true winner: "I'm scared."

What father is going to force his child to stay in her room while witches fly back and forth over her bed? It's hard for me to be a stickler for bedtime when she's afraid because I've been there myself. As a kid, my biggest bedtime fear was … boogers. They lived under the bed. During the day they were harmless dustballs that tumbled with the slightest breeze. At sundown they started clumping together, and by bedtime you had a full-blown malicious booger lying under the bed, waiting for you to drop an arm or leg over the side.

My cousins and I discussed boogers at great length, especially when we were spending the night at my grandfather's house, the booger hotel of southern Anderson County. Papa and Granny lived in an old farmhouse that was full of excellent hiding places for boogers: latched closets, dim hallways, a back bedroom with a hole in the ceiling through which boogers were free to come and go as they pleased. And the yard teemed with booger hideouts: in tumbledown barns, behind the outhouse, or in the perpetual twilight under the worn planks of the front porch.

Getting ourselves scared to death was one of the funnest things in the world to do. In the middle of a bright summer afternoon under a protective benevolent sun, talk of boogers was not scary at all; toward suppertime, such talk became a little more exciting; by dusk, it was terrifying.

After supper, when the sun slipped below the horizon, we took to the yard to play "Ain't No Boogers Out Tonight." The game was a variation of hide and seek. One of us would find a good hiding place, and the rest of us, after counting to twenty-five, ventured out, holding hands and repeating a singsong refrain:

Ain't no boogers out tonight.
Papa killed 'em all last night!

When the seekers were perilously far from the safety of base, the booger sprang from his hiding place, and shrieking cousins scattered like chickens fleeing a rabid cow.

We enjoyed the thrill of being scared to death, but not one of us looked forward to the next time we'd have to sleep alone. That's when the real boogers came out—the ones that waited under the bed or snuck out of the closet and hid in the shadowy pile of clothes on the floor between you and the door.

The only cure for a booger encounter was for your parents to come into your room, turn on the light and do a booger sweep. "See? There are no boogers in this room. You had a bad dream. Go back to sleep." (But I wasn't asleep!) Even after your parents promise that boogers aren't real, you still can't sleep. Everybody knows they reappear the moment your dad starts snoring again.

So I try to be understanding when my little girl tells me she is afraid. Because sometimes, late at night, when a mournful hound and I are the only two creatures awake in the whole world, I'm pretty sure I hear a chuckle coming from under the bed.

Intensive Care

I'm hurting. It's been less than three hours since I've undergone oral surgery, and I'm not feeling too good. Part of my mouth is numb, and when I try to sip a Pepsi it dribbles down my chin and onto my shirt. Another part of my mouth feels like mush. I am feeling sorry for myself. I am being self-indulgent, but I feel I have earned the right.

My wife is somewhere else in the house, doing house stuff. She is not hovering over me and making reassuring cooing sounds. During the surgery she went out for a burger and shopping at K-Mart. She brought me home and left me in bed with a bowl of Jello. I am abandoned.

Suddenly, our three-year-old bounds into the room, home from daycare. She rushes to my side. She is concerned. How sweet! She wants to be reassured Daddy is not going to die.

"Can I see where you got a shot?" she asks.

I show her the puff of cotton taped to my arm.

"Wow!"

Satisfied, she is gone.

Our immensely more mature almost-six-year-old strolls by on her way to something more important. I sigh with heartfelt dejection, catching her attention.

"Oh, hi, Daddy," she says. Her smile brightens the room. "How are you feeling?"

"Mflgah," I reply.

Wonderful child, I think. At least she cares about me. She comes to my side.

"Daddy, can I see your stitches?"

"Mflgah," I say, nodding weakly.

I strain to open my mouth, only I can't tell how far it's open because I can't feel it. I drool onto my person. My daughter peers inside my mouth for a moment, studying the situation.

"Mflgah?" I ask.

"Gross, Daddy," she replies, shaking her head.

And then she leaves, too. I hear her tell her mother that Daddy has Jello on his shirt.

The next morning, in the whirl of getting ready for work and playschool, my children are sent to me for goodbye kisses.

"Daddy, can I see where you got your shot?" asks the three-year-old.

I hold out my arm. The bandage has been removed, to her keen disappointment. She bursts into tears and runs from the room. She doesn't even kiss me goodbye.

The mature almost-six-year-old rolls her eyes, as if to let me know she, too, doesn't understand kids today.

"Can I see your stitches?" she asks.

I oblige, again. She cranes for the best possible view, frowning and shaking her head during the examination.

"Daddy," she finally says, "why do you have bracelets on your teeth?"

"Mflgah."

She kisses me on the cheek and leaves.

Good question.

Number Two and Trying Harder

There are certain advantages to being the firstborn. For one thing, you get your picture taken a lot. You never have to wonder if you might have been adopted, as my wife's sister did. Debbie was the firstborn, and there exist hundreds of photographs to prove it. See Debbie just minutes after she was born! See Debbie try to eat her first blanket! See Debbie throw up on the blanket! See Debbie's naked-baby picture, the one in which she is crying because she knows her mother will show the photograph to her friends when she is a teenager!

Beth was the second child. Taking pictures of red, wrinkled, crying infants had lost its charm by then, so precious few photographs exist to prove that Beth was really born. Her physical existence as a toddler has been called into question, although scientists from Polaroid have positively identified hers as the leg sticking out from behind a closet door her sister tries to close it in an early-1960s snapshot.

Beth was convinced she was adopted, a theory her older sister felt the need to reinforce. When the sisters looked through the family photo album, young Beth would point to a picture of her older sister throwing up on a blanket and laugh. Debbie would smile and say, "Beth, did you know that you were adopted?" which ended the fun right then and there.

It took years to get her straightened out, but now Beth is married and raising two happy, well-adjusted, quiet, docile, obedient, problem-free, perfect children of her own. She has lots of pictures of the first one. The second one was born recently, so we must wait to see if she has learned from her childhood trauma and will take measures to make sure her second-born doesn't think Mommy and Daddy love big brother more.

The first child often gets the lion's share of the glory. As the father of two daughters, I must plead guilty. There are two large boxes of nothing-but-Katie pictures. I've got enough stuff to scare away boyfriends for twenty years. As I look up, I see a photo of Katie in my arms the day after she was born ... a digitized computer picture of Katie at the county fair ... two drawings that Katie made for me.

When Amy comes into my office she sometimes points to the pictures and says, "Look, Daddy—there's Katie!" I recoil in guilt. There is but one small picture of Amy on my desk, and it was made when she was one. (Even that single photograph shares a frame with one of Katie.)

Pictures aren't my only offenses. As I review the columns I've written—thinking about Katie's impending birth was the reason I started writing—I see that Katie's childhood has been chronicled in the local weekly paper. In this space I told about her birth, her antics, her fears, her letters to Santa, her first night spent away from home. But there is very little I've written that's been exclusively Amy. Even here, again, she has had to share space with her older sister.

It would be easy to feel sorry for her if it weren't for the fact that God has granted a special dispensation to all second-born children that empowers them to make life agony for older brothers and sisters. Second children are God's way of making sure firstborns don't grow up feeling too self-important. Katie may be the first, but Amy makes her pay dearly for the privilege. Some of her tactics include putting beans in her sister's Kool-Aid, changing the clothes on her sister's Barbies without permission, singing with Katie when she doesn't want to be sung with, sleeping in Katie's bed, not closing her mouth when she chews, and generally kicking, gouging and screaming and being a real pain. She is excellent at this.

She is good at other things, too, like telling Katie she looks pretty in her new Sunday dress, or sharing a fun bath time, or playing model to her sister's latest fashion ideas, or sharing her bicycle with Katie because Katie likes Amy's bicycle better, or asking interesting questions like, "How time is it?"

She is also good at rocking. It falls upon me to rock her to sleep every night, a practice some would say I should have abandoned a couple of years ago. But the time we spend in the rocker just before she closes her eyes on the day is as important to me as it is to her. We have an understanding. It is our time—a chance for us to communicate through the creaking of the rocker, through strokes and pats and lullabies and, sometimes, whispered conversation:

"Amy, did you see that airplane today?"

"Yes."

"Have you ever flown in an airplane?"

"Yes."

"You did? When?"

"When I was in a dream."

Sweet dreams, honey. This one's for you.

Back-to-School Blues

There they are, in their Batman tee shirts, sunglasses, high-top basketball shoes and yellow instruction sheets, all looking very cool.

These members of the latest crop of college freshmen wander the halls, consulting their instructions and squinting upward for some sign over a door, anything that might tell them where they are. They move uncertain about campus, their eyes glazing over. Freshman shock. Put a bunch of eighteen-year-olds in a room and give them yellow instruction sheets, and the whole thing grinds to a halt.

They'll be fine in a few days. By the time they realize the

underwear fairy isn't swooping into their dorm rooms with fresh Fruit of the Looms, the healing process has begun.

This year, the arrival of students at the college where I work coincides with my daughter's first day of school. She is starting first grade, which is a pretty big deal for a six-year-old—and her parents.

For several weeks the conversation around our house has been sprinkled with comments about the big event. We'll be eating supper, and all of a sudden one of us will say, "Katie's going to be in the first grade!" which causes her to grin and float upward on a rising thermal of superiority, from where she looks downward on her younger sister.

Imagine my surprise when, on the night before the first day of school, I found Katie fighting back tears in her bed. Her mom had already tipped me to the possibility of some pre-first-grade anxiety, but I wasn't expecting tears—not from the kid who owned preschool and kindergarten. She told me her stomach was hurting and she was crying because she was afraid her stomach would hurt the next day in school.

When I asked if she was worried about moving up to first grade, she said she was sad because she wouldn't know anybody there. I told her she already knew many of the children who would be in her class, but she seemed more concerned about the ones she didn't know.

"What if I fall down and they all laugh at me?" she asked.

She told me her kindergarten teacher, Mrs. Maynard, always allowed her to go to the bathroom whenever she asked. She talked about the sandbox in Mrs. Maynard's room and the broom she and her friends would use to sweep up spilled sand. It pleased her that Mrs. Maynard would trust them with the responsibility. She told me they could play on anything in the playground, a privilege not granted to all the other classes.

She was expressing something I didn't know she was old enough to feel—something like homesickness. Tomorrow morning she was going to leave the safety of home and embark on something new—a new teacher, new classmates, an unknown, frightening new world.

I fumbled for the right words: "You'll see lots of your old friends … you'll make new friends very fast … first grade will be lots of fun … you will love your new teacher!"

She forced a smile, as though to let me know she appreciated my attempt to comfort her but this was something she had to handle for herself. For maybe the first time since I've been her father, I felt helpless.

"Okay?" I asked.

"Okay. 'Night, Daddy."

"Goodnight, honey."

They say the best we can do for our kids is to raise them so that someday they won't need us anymore. But part of me would rather see her ask for my help than suck it up and tackle first grade all by herself. I don't want my little girl to feel like she has to be brave. I'd rather build a wall around her to shield her from everything that's scary.

But I won't do that. Instead, I'll drop her off at school tomorrow and every day for the next too-few years and watch her walk into the building—she and her friends in their Batman tee shirts, sunglasses and high-top basketball shoes, all looking very cool.

It's the right thing to do, which makes me wonder why it feels so hard.

This Old Yard

I don't have a strong background in horticulture. I used to think a crepe myrtle was something with ice cream on top. With that disclaimer, I plunge headlong into an advice column on a subject for which K-Mart has seen fit to create an entire department: lawn and garden care.

First, let's drop the garden part. The sequence of the words—lawn, followed by garden—implies that one should have a requisite working knowledge of lawn care before taking up the mysteries of squash reproduction. So let's can the tomatoes for now.

This instructional offering is intended for the young homeowner who wants to be sure his will be the ugliest, most pitiful lawn in the whole subdivision. Do you want a yard where rocks belch forth from the earth overnight? Is it important that your lawn provide a haven for endangered species of bugs, worms and rabbit droppings? Does your spine tingle when a tentacle of crabgrass wraps itself around your ankle? If you answered yes to any of these questions, welcome aboard.

Let's talk equipment. You should go out and spend more than two thousand dollars for a riding lawnmower, preferably one with a fancy name, like the Whacker High Vac Super Torque Sucker Upper. Remember, you get what you pay for, and a really bad lawn doesn't come cheap. It's a proud moment for the whole family the first time you crank up the brand-new Whacker and take a few turns around the yard, even if you take out a cat and the gas grill in the process. You have made a good investment. Be good to your machine, and your machine will be good to you. Spend more time with your machine than you do with your kids. You and your machine are one. Say it. Good. Again.

Ah, but slow down, Grasshopper. Before you can mow the lawn, you need to grow the lawn. First, go to the bank and get a loan. Next, go to K-Mart (not a feed-and-seed store, where they know about these things) and buy a lot of Kentucky-31 grass seed, which will grow in Kentucky but not where you live. Remember, the point is not to have a nice lawn, but to coax in all the vagrant weeds hanging around the edge of your yard and looking like trouble just waiting to happen. Kentucky-31 is a real help here. You plant it, and it pops up green and plush. Soon the juvenile-delinquent weeds start sneaking in at night to see what all the fun is. One morning you wake up to find that the Kentucky-31 has left town. Congratulations! You have succeeded in attracting a healthy variety of weeds to your yard. You are now ready to decapitate them with the Whacker.

It is important to note here that a really bad lawn requires more than just watering, fertilizing and mowing. Anyone can do that.

What a successful bad lawn needs most is the personal touch. Just as some people talk to their houseplants, it is important, while astride your machine, to speak to your lawn. The most effective communication will include insults loud enough to be heard above the roar of your Briggs & Stratton: "You stupid crabgrass! You make me sick! This is the ugliest yard in the universe! You are not a credit to the community! I disown you!" Stuff like that really turns crabgrass on, and soon it will multiply spontaneously when it hears you start the machine. Within a few short weeks you'll have crabgrass coming up between the cracks in your driveway. (And you thought it would be difficult.)

Once you have established a fine stand of weedery, you should think of planting shrubbery, which people do because they don't want other people to see where their houses touch the ground. Like the pale section of ankle between the top of a man's sock and the bottom of his trousers, it's unsightly, and to leave it exposed too long is just not done.

But we don't want that, do we? No! Let's get to work.

Gentlemen, start your engines!

Getting Ready for 2001

Our six-year-old daughter, the first-grader, walked into the kitchen the other night and informed us that the Grand Canyon stretches across three states.

"That's great, honey," said we, the beaming parents of a brilliant child. "Which three states?"

"A red one, a blue one and I don't remember the color of the other one."

Geographic nitpicking aside, she is a learning machine, and sometimes she amazes me. Anything that crosses her line of sight is at risk of being read: books, cereal boxes, billboards—anything with words, stuff most of us never bother with. Do you know what the printing on the inside of your shoe says? Katie does.

She has a good memory, too. Don't tell her you're going to take her to the video store unless you mean it, because she will remind you. Her mind is a miniature black hole that sucks up any piece of information that drifts by. Inside her head is an efficient filing system that puts everything in logical order and then, when needed, whisks it to the surface. At six, her mind is many million times more complex than the computers that pilot the Space Shuttle.

Parents magazine reminds us that young children soak up knowledge like a sponge and that half of everything a person knows, he or she learned before the age of ten. That puts a lot of pressure on parents, who feel obligated to stuff the wisdom of the ages into a brain the size of a small cantaloupe. We do this because we want our children to have every possible advantage when they are grown. Knowing that the Grand Canyon covers two of the three primary colors may prove to be important in the next millennium.

We're preparing our kids for life in the twenty-first century. Just saying those words—the twenty-first century—conjures up an image of George Jetson zipping around the stratosphere in his nuclear-powered bubble car. But we don't know what the future will bring. A generation ago, could my parents have imagined such things as VCRs, microwave ovens, car phones or Japanese banks owning most of America? The future will always surprise, so we strive to give our kids a solid base of knowledge from which to work.

In my quest to create intellectually superior yet otherwise perfectly normal children, I have found it to be true: trash in, trash out. Children are consistent—if you utter something in their presence, sooner or later it will come back to you. For instance, when they say, "In a minute," or, "Huh," or, "Why do I have to do everything around here?" you can bet they learned it from a grownup. By the same token, when they look a stranger in the eye and recite the principles of global economic stability, you can wink at your spouse and take credit for that, too.

The danger is that you can take it to an extreme. You know you're pushing too hard when your kids start bickering over the Pythagorean Theorem. I hate it when they do that. Also, if you are tempted to laminate the flash cards so they can practice their vowels while taking a bath, you probably should let them ride bikes instead.

It's all about balance. I recently was thinking pretty good thoughts about how healthy my balance was when my breathless three-year-old ran to me with pen and paper in hand and asked, "Daddy, how do you spell S?"

Well.

Growing Pains

Every weekday morning, after we cross the railroad tracks and turn left toward the street where her school is, Katie, our six-year-old, unbuckles her seatbelt and gives us a goodbye kiss. We pull up to the curb and wish her a good day, and she hops out of the car and sprints toward her school without a backward glance.

If it's Monday, Wednesday, or Friday, we then drive Amy, the three-year-old, to her Aunt Vivi's house, where she will wait for her grandmother to come and take her to preschool. Like her older sister, she is eager to escape the confines of the back seat and get on with the business of having fun. Sometimes we have to tackle her to get a peck on the cheek. The routine is similar on Tuesdays and Thursdays, when we take Amy to Miss Lou's. She no longer requires a parental escort to the front door; instead, we let her off at the sidewalk and watch until she is safely inside. The last thing we see before driving away is the bouncing backside of a tiny pair of Levi's—Miss Independent, full speed ahead.

Long gone are the days when I had to pry my clinging children from my leg. I felt guilty about leaving them to go to work. It was for a worthwhile cause, I reasoned—food and clothing and roof-over-their-heads kind of stuff—but I still felt guilty.

Sometimes, when we drive away from Miss Lou's, Amy stands on tiptoe to look out the window. We can only see her from the eyes up. We wave, but she doesn't respond, probably because she's using both hands to pull herself up. We also can't tell if she's smiling, but we doubt it. We drive away—two guilt-ridden, thirty-something parents just trying to provide for their kids. Her eyes haunt us the rest of the day.

A variation of the haunting-eyes routine is the double-haunting-eyes, which happens when we leave both children at the same place. Picture again the half-obscured head of Amy with her staring eyes ... add to that the taller Katie, looking forlornly out the window, one hand signing "I love you." It's a double dose of guilt.

But they don't do that as often as they used to. Katie is in first grade, and that means she can't wait to see her friends each morning. I don't believe it has ever occurred to her to look back after she gets out of the car. She disappears into that classroom to do things I will never be able to share in. When I ask her how her day was, she says, "Fine." When I ask her what she studied, she says, "Oh, math and stuff." How was lunch? "Good." What did you have? "I don't remember."

When I ask Amy how her day went, she launches into an animated account of how Lucas (not his real name) threw dirt in her face and how she cried but not too much. Despite the drama, she relates the story with enthusiasm. She apparently understands the attack to be one of the rites of passage for preschoolers. Bring on the Lucases of the world!

I'm not so comfortable with the fact that my children are beginning to show signs of independence, although I know it's my job to make sure they do. I must give them a little line every time they feel the need to try something on their own, but I tug gently to remind them I'm still there if they should need me. Little by little, they learn to do things on their own. Their confidence grows, and they grow, and that's good. Because one day they will drive away, and I will be the one who stands at the window and watches.

The Stick

There are many cool things that go along with being a parent: You get to teach your kid how to ride a bike, it's okay to watch cartoons and go to Disney movies, and you're allowed to roll around on the floor and grunt like a rhinoceros. You also get to eat at McDonald's. A lot.

It is fun living in the same house with little humans, but not always, especially when they get sick. When I picked up Amy on a Friday afternoon and found her languishing in Miss Lou's arms, I knew she was sick. She was running a fever and her throat hurt. We gave her Tylenol and decided to take her to the pediatrician on Saturday morning if she wasn't feeling better.

She wasn't, and so began the adventure. After we arrived at the doctor's office, she told me in exact terms that anyone dressed in white and holding a needle was not to be allowed near her.

"No shots," she said.

"Honey, I don't think you're going to get a shot," I said with all the reassurance I could muster.

"And I don't want him to put The Stick in my throat," she continued.

I hesitated, knowing I couldn't guarantee he wouldn't use The Stick. Before I could respond, she moved on to her next demand. "Daddy, I don't want to get up on that table. You can hold me."

"Honey, don't worry, I'll think the doctor wil—"

Suddenly the door flew open and the tall man himself swept into the room. "Good morning!" he said all too cheerfully. Amy's fevered muscles snapped to attention. Ten fingers dug into my shoulders. When he offered her a Christmas teddy-bear sticker, she recoiled, then warily accepted it. With little fanfare, the doctor, a real pro, moved smoothly to the examination, initiating a game of Does This Tickle with his stethoscope. Amy countered with a ploy of her own: the good-doctor, good-patient strategy. He asked if her throat hurt. She shook her head no while I nodded yes. She faked a smile, chattering about this and that, pretending she wasn't scared. She hoped to sidetrack him enough to make him forget about The Stick.

Things were going pretty smoothly. If you were the patient, you might have thought the worst was over because the doctor was talking to Daddy now. Suddenly, without warning, he turned and reached for the drawer that held THE STICK! Amy had seen this movie before. She climbed me like a tree. I held her flailing legs while the doctor did his duty. It was over in a moment. Her throat was swabbed and he was out the door to run a test. She sobbed for a minute; I held her tight and promised it was over.

In a few minutes the doctor came back to tell us Amy did indeed have a strep infection.

"That's what I was afraid of," I said. "Her sister had it two weeks ago. In fact, I may have to go to the doctor myself."

He spun around from writing a prescription and looked at me. "Does your throat hurt?" he demanded.

"Uh-oh," said Amy.

"Just … little," I stammered, whereupon he reached into the drawer, pulled out The Stick, and JABBED IT INTO MY MOUTH!

"Open wide!"

"Ahhhhhhhhh … arggggghhhh … yuck!"

I tried not to behave like a baby in front of my child, who watched in wonderment as the tables were turned. When the doctor was done, he told me I could make his next car payment on my way out. Then he ducked under the doorway and was gone, swooping off to impart fear and dread.

Amy, no longer crying, took my hand.

"You were very brave, Daddy," she said. "We can go to McDonald's."

Predictions for 1990

I couldn't help but notice at the grocery checkout—as I waited to pay for milk, bread and eggs in eager anticipation of snowstorms foretold by highly skilled weather people—that ten famous psychics have come out with their predictions for the coming year.

As I scanned the headlines of some finer examples of journalism, I learned that in 1990 Eddie Murphy will give birth to an alien lovechild, and Nancy will divorce Ronnie and run off with Gorbachev. Like a buzzard to road kill, I was engrossed.

I also was struck that people are paid huge sums of money to say these things. So, this being the land of opportunity, I have decided to become a famous psychic, too. You can help me achieve this Great American Dream by encouraging the publisher of this newspaper to pay me huge sums of money. However, my first prediction for 1990 is that the publisher will not pay me huge sums of money. I am sensing extremely negative vibes in regard to that. But this should not prevent you from following through on an impulse to run to the Post Office and mail me fifty dollars or more.

Anyway, for free, here are my predictions for 1990:

• Charlie Gertz—and I'm really going out on a limb here—will forecast snow, and it will instead be sunny and seventy-two degrees. Call me crazy.

• My youngest child will pick her nose 456 times, and her older sister will report the infraction 457 times—one extra for the time she probably did it when no one was looking.

• My wife will start thirty-seven cross-stitch projects. I also predict she will kill me if I make any jokes about how many she will finish.

• I will not win the Publishers Clearing House Sweepstakes.

• No grass will grow in my yard this spring, and I will open a factory outlet for red clay.

• I will spend many hours hitting little white balls into uncharted woodland areas.

• Every time I go into one of two vacant bathrooms in my house, little children will be drawn to the door, where they will tap and ask if anyone is in there.

• My wife and I will go out to eat without our children once in the coming year, and, out of habit, she will request twenty extra napkins.

• An unfortunate shopper will ignore K-Mart's advisory to make her final selections and move to the front and will never be heard from again.

• Dance schools and classic-car clubs will be banned from Christmas parades, leaving only politicians and vendors pushing shopping carts filled with balloons and cotton candy.

• The amount of money my wife spends on children's clothes in 1990 will eclipse the national debt.

• Somebody, in a momentary state of boredom, will pick up his phone, dial his own number and hang up very fast to see if it will ring.

• My family will set a new world's record for the amount of garbage that can be stacked above the rim of a trash can.

• I will make the third payment on the pediatrician's Mercedes by August.

• A strange new life form will emerge from the murky depths of a Tupperware container that has lurked on a back shelf of our refrigerator for the past several months.

• And, my final prediction: My wife will arrange for me to sleep in the storage building when she reads this stuff.

Invasion of the Minivans

There's a conspiracy brewing at our house. The women who live here have decided that what this family needs is a minivan.

Of course there's nothing wrong with owning a minivan—if you enjoy driving a Kelvinator refrigerator with wheels. Minivans are the ultimate in cute, which is my wife's primary reason for wanting one. "I like the way this model looks," she says in utter seriousness, completely ignoring other factors, such as price. She also ignores the fact that her favorite minivan is built by the same motor company I have sworn never to patronize even if she hangs me upside down till my eyeballs bug out.

"You can't buy a vehicle simply because it's cute," say I, the proud former owner of a perky little lime-green Chevy Vega with Mag wheels and a stacked-up rear end.

At this point in the discussion, her tactical instincts kick in, and she argues that the minivan is a very practical vehicle for today's on-the-go family.

"But we already have a practical family car," I counter, referring, of course, to the 1977 Oldsmobile Delta 88 Custom Cruiser Family Truckster Station Wagon (Limited Edition). I can look out the kitchen window and see it reposing in all its glory: blue with woodgrain siding (well, it used to look like woodgrain siding), a little faded on the hood (not unlike the graying temples of a venerable college professor), 130,000 miles on the odometer and still going strong (well, technically, still going). It is a fine automobile.

The Family Truckster was built when cars were cars, men were men, and the word minivan sounded like a contradiction in terms, like jumbo shrimp and congressional ethics.

There are many advantages to owning a mature vehicle like the Family Truckster. For instance, when you drive this behemoth down the street, people in minivans pull their vehicles over to the side of the road. These drivers are showing respect for a classic automobile and not, as my wife insists, trying to protect their precious minivans from the Truckster.

Not that the Family Truckster couldn't hold its own in a dustup. Make no mistake: No matter how sleek her lines, the Truckster is a Sherman tank with a luggage rack. BMWs have been known to take their chances with the guard rail when confronted with a sudden lane shift by the Truckster.

Another advantage to owning a fine vehicle like the Family Truckster is that it doubles as a mobile storage unit for the children. When we take the kids to school, church or grandma's house, they carry all the dolls, pocketbooks, pads and crayons they can scoop up on the way out the door. Then they dump this stuff in the floor of the car, where it fossilizes under the intense pressure of more dolls, pocketbooks, pads and crayons. When your child wants to know what happened to the ant farm she got for Christmas, you reply, "I don't know, honey. Have you looked in the Pleistocene layer?"

The trump card is that the Family Truckster is paid for, an argument even my wife has a hard time countering.

"You're probably right," she concedes, even as she and the other two female persons in our house retreat to plot their next offensive.

We don't want a minivan. Someone help me. Please.

Raising Tomorrow's Woman

As an educational service, we present a primer on raising the well-prepared daughter. Our basic tenet is simple: Start young. It is never too early to begin preparing your young lady for life's realities. Here are some steps you can take to be sure she is ready to be a woman of the twenty-first century.

- Dance lessons. One of the most important things you can do is enroll your daughter in dance lessons. There will be numerous times later in her adult life (Christmas parties, Sunday school picnics and other social gatherings) when her mother and other well-meaning friends will ask her to perform the cute little tap routine she spent nine months learning when she was six. One should be prepared to apply for a student loan in order to pay for leotards, tap shoes, ballet slippers, leg warmers, tote bags, uniforms, tights, jackets, lessons, photos, and recital and competition fees. But it'll all be worth it when she masters that winsome dance routine, "Splish, Splash, I Was Taking a Bath." Culture can be bought.

- Barbie dolls. We cannot stress enough the importance of maintaining an amply stocked stable of Barbie dolls for your Little Miss. Besides the obvious advantage of elevating your daughter's fashion consciousness, today's Barbie serves as a role model for Tomorrow's

Woman. With today's emphasis on good physical health, Barbie shines like a beacon through the fog, reminding young ladies everywhere that what's really important in life is a nine-inch waistline. As an added incentive, Barbie can do splits, which encourages your daughter to pursue those dance lessons.

• Reeboks. It goes without saying that today's girl needs brand-name footwear. It is a parent's responsibility to stay current in the ever-changing world of sneakerdom. What's hot today may be passé tomorrow. L.A. Gear is hot. I think.

• Lunchboxes. As long as your daughter's lunchbox is adorned with images of Barbie, New Kids on the Block or some other acceptable celebrity, you are fulfilling your duty. Also under this category fall purses, sweatshirts and backpacks.

• Fruit Loops. Thanks to the power of Saturday morning television, your daughter is prepared to decide which breakfast cereal you should buy her. A helpful tip for parents: If the cereal has a cartoon character on the box and contains seventy-five percent sugar, you're safe. Buy with confidence.

• Golden Arches. The McDonald's business model has come to symbolize today's generation of young women: Make them all exactly the same. It's no wonder we frequent the Golden Arches with our daughters to partake of the balanced and nutritious meals offered there. McDonald's is a hap-hap-happy place, and your daughter's psyche is not something to trifle with. Buy her a Happy Meal and you will sleep better tonight.

• Multiple bathrooms. Women who live together under the

same roof tend to congregate in a single bathroom for their beauty regimens. Still, your daughter should have her own bathroom so that the father will have a place to brush his teeth and shave. By doing this, he contributes in a small way to the female bonding process.

• Sibling diplomacy. Raising one perfect daughter is not enough for some parents, so they leap into the waters of multiple childship. One thing they discover, however, is that siblings don't always like each other. The older child knows everything and has little tolerance for a baby sister who knows nothing. The baby learns to play this bias like a Stradivarius. She walks away unimpressed when her older sister tries to lay some wisdom on her, leaving a perfectionist seething in her wake. Encourage these frank exchanges. They will come in handy when your daughters have kids of their own and present you with the satisfying opportunity to say, "See? I tried to tell you."

Long Live Chicken Little

I don't know how people sleep at night. Last October, I came across the following headline buried in the newspaper, right next to Dear Abby: "Satellite to Come Down Flaming in November." This headline appeared in a bona fide daily newspaper, not one of those publications we pretend not to read in the grocery store while waiting for the checkout person to take our loan application. The story went on to describe how a huge satellite called Solar Max was about to fall from the sky "possibly in three big chunks," to repeat the scientific terms used in the Associated Press article.

I shared this alarming information with my family and received mixed reactions. Amy, four, rushed outside and parked her bicycle under the protective eaves of the house. My wife, ever the opportunist, wanted to know if someone could calculate exactly where the fiery satellite would crash to Earth so she could park the station wagon there. Six-year-old Katie seconded her mother's idea and suggested we shoot the whole thing with a camcorder and send it off to America's Funniest Home Videos and win ten thousand dollars.

I had hoped for a more thoughtful response. Even my coworkers failed to grasp the gravity of the situation. They thought of any number of places they would enjoy seeing obliterated by three big chunks of satellite parts.

The article warned us to expect the imminent reentry of the satellite in November. I followed the newspaper carefully and watched the news for several months afterwards, but never again was there any mention of the wayward satellite. Nothing. Not even on CNN.

Perhaps it was a practical joke. Another article I read described how astronomers have discovered what they believe to be the oldest object in the universe—a quasar that is eighty-two trillion billion miles from Earth. How did they know it was old? "If you look carefully in the lower left-hand corner," said Dr. John Sleighter, gazing through the Mount Palomar Observatory telescope, "you can just make out a little bumper sticker that says, 'Let me tell you about my grandchildren.'"

Oh, those wacky theoretical physicists!

Demon Waitress from Pluto

It was a dark and stormy night. (It was really a sunny afternoon, but an ominous setting is better for this horror story.) Gather your children close. Shutter the windows and hang a sprig of garlic on the doorpost. Prepare to hear the story of ... The Demon Waitress from Pluto.

It all started quietly enough. A young couple with two and a half kids, a station wagon and a mortgage decided to dine out for Sunday lunch. If they had known what awaited them, they would have ordered takeout from the Colonel instead.

When they passed through the door of the seafood restaurant, they saw a line. There had never been a line before. It was one o'clock when they were seated and got their first look at the Demon Waitress from Pluto. She seemed normal enough, but don't they always?

The waitress gave the children crayons and paper placemats and smiled while the parents tried to get their daughters to say with their physical mouths, yes or no, if they wanted the chicken fingers, instead of rolling their eyes back in their heads and acting as though they had never been in a public place. Yes, finally, the children would have the chicken fingers, and could they have some hushpuppies while they waited for their meals? The waitress promised to be back with hushpuppies in thirty seconds, which is Plutonian for "not in a lifetime of your earth-days."

When the hushpuppies and salads failed to materialize after ten minutes, the father conjectured that the waitress had forgotten, which was a reasonable assumption—assuming she was human. Several minutes later, he managed to flag her down. Before he could utter a word she flashed a chilling grin and promised that the hushpuppies were forthcoming. Then she was gone. A pair of kitchen doors flapped in her wake, the only evidence she had visited them.

Later, at a point when time had lost all meaning, she produced exactly four stunted hushpuppies, which the family devoured like starving wolf pups. The father looked across the restaurant and observed that a family who had entered the restaurant with them had finished dessert and was preparing to go home and enjoy a leisurely Sunday afternoon. They are so lucky, he thought. A miserable lone hushpuppy growled resentfully from deep within him.

The older daughter, a meticulous crayon artist, had finished her placemat masterpiece, had it framed and arranged for a showing at a downtown gallery. She lay snoring on the table. The younger daughter had stopped crying and was under the table sifting for crumbs.

When forty-five minutes had passed and there was still no food on the table, the father kind-of-demanded that his family be served, whereupon the waitress babbled furiously in an extraterrestrial tongue and retreated to the kitchen. She reappeared with plates that appeared to have passed within the general vicinity of a microwave oven.

The young family choked down stiff chicken fingers and half-fried shrimp, then fled the restaurant because the Demon Waitress from Pluto and her companions were roosting by the beverage station, speaking in whispers, occasionally scanning the room to make sure the remaining diners were all still out of iced tea.

Sometime after two o'clock the family emerged, shaken, from the dark hole of their personal Twilight Zone. But even in the safety of the parking lot, in the bright midday warmth, a cold dread inched its way up their spines. And so it was that later that afternoon, Raymond Floyd inexplicably jerked a shot into the murky waters guarding the eleventh hole at Augusta National, blowing the lead and losing the Master's Tournament.

Your move, Stephen King.

The Competition

The lights in the cavernous hall begin to fade, and the drone of a thousand conversations rises, reaching a cheering crescendo as the supple young dancer strides to center stage and commands the spotlight.

There she stands, the starlet, absorbing the adoration of hundreds of young girls who would gladly sell a sibling to be like her. Her sequins beam hope back into the faces of her worshipers. After a full minute, she lifts the microphone. The crowd falls silent.

"Good afternoon, dancers, teachers and parents, and welcome to the third annual Wish-Upon-a-Falling-Star Regional Dance Competition, where young dancers can pursue the all-American dream to grow up and dance in a Janet Jackson music video."

The crowd erupts. A father balances his bouncing leotard-clad three-year-old on his shoulders. Mothers from rival dance schools, their fists pumping, chant their schools' names. The fever of competition sears the air. With a willowy sweep of her arm, the starlet subdues the crowd.

"I know you have worked long and hard to get here. Dancers, you've practiced your routine day after day in order to perfect it for the three minutes you will be in the spotlight at this, the Wish-Up-on-a-Falling-Star Regional Dance Competition. But isn't it worth it all? Why pursue an empty goal like appreciation for the arts? What good is it if you can't use it? Competition is all!"

The audience rises as one. Their cheers buffet the stage curtain. The starlet feeds on her devotees' energy. She glides to stage left, and a mother faints.

"And you, parents: You've invested hundreds of dollars in lessons, costumes, shoes, competition fees (and may I mention that the ten-dollar entry fee you have paid will go only to defray expenses and don't think for a minute we're only in this for the money) just to make it to this important moment in your child's career. And, yes, I do mean career, parents. What happens today could well determine your child's future. Who knows when the big break might come? Who knows when someone from that show might see your precious little one on the community-service cable channel? Do you know the show of which I speak?"

"YES!" the crowd roars.

"Dare I say the name of the television program that has come to symbolize for our children the realization of a dream?" she teases.

"YES!" they scream.

"Oh, really—shall I tell you?"

Rabid fans stomp and chant, "TELL US! TELL US! TELL US!"

The spotlight operator, his sense of timing honed by years of experience, drops in an orange filter, and the young starlet is suddenly—startlingly—bathed in gold. In full majesty, she looks upon her subjects. The audience gasps. The intensity is too much for some; paramedics work the aisles. Misty eyes track the starlet's every move. She surveys the auditorium. Finally satisfied that every inch of the room belongs to her, she lifts the microphone.

And she says,

"Star Search."

It is reported that instruments detected "significant seismic activity" in the city. Worried scientists noted that earthquakes are extremely rare for the region.

How We Roll

In our quest to keep you informed of the best in family entertainment, we present: bowling.

Yes, bowling—a pastime where you try to avoid crushing your big toe with a spheroid of equal mass to a minor planet while attempting to propel the same spheroid down a narrow wooden lane exposed on either side by evil traps.

Safe and fun, right?

Bowling is also the only activity that affords you the opportunity to wear shoes that have shared the soles, and I mean this literally, of hundreds of other people. Bowling lore suggests that the phrase, "Walk a mile in my shoes," was first spoken by factory worker Hiram Butz when he bowled thirty-two straight games after a twelve-hour shift at the compost plant.

While you are waiting your turn to bowl, you might make a sport of imagining who the milestone wearers of your shoes were—for instance, the 500th wearer, the wearer with the highest average, the wearer with the sweatiest feet, or the percentage of wearers who were Methodists.

Another shoe game one might try is "I Spy," where you say something like, "I spy something red," and your children say, "Your shoe!" and then you say, "I spy something blue," and they say, "Your shoe!"

"I spy something with pizza on it!"

"YOUR SHOE!"

And so forth.

Such games are a great diversion, because there's not much else to do while you wait for your turn to bowl. This wasn't always the case. Before the invention of computerized scorekeeping, it was up to human beings to master the tricky mathematics of this exercise. Back in the day, you needed a pencil and a pad and old-fashioned brain power to keep up with the score. For instance, if you were lucky enough to get a strike in the third frame, you figured your score based on your next frame, minus the sea level of the city where you were born, multiplied by the date of Elvis's last sighting. The shortcut to this formula was just to put down a home run, which is what I usually did.

Scorekeeping aside, bowling is an activity in which the whole family can participate, and it's cheap. At the place where we bowl, kids roll for free. We walk up to the counter to put down a deposit on our rental shoes (so that we won't be tempted to steal them), and the man asks my daughter how old she is. "Six," she says with pride. "Why, we've got shoes older than that!" he says, laughing. "Free bowling for you!"

We go to our lane and begin putting on our shoes, and we notice that the proprietors have been thoughtful enough to put numbers on the heels so that we won't get our shoes mixed up. Amy, our four-year-old, is up first. She jogs to the edge of the lane, stops, and drops her ball. It sits there like a stunned animal, obviously in shock. A few minutes later we sense that it has begun to rotate very slowly in the general direction of the pins. Amy, bored, does cartwheels. Her sister rolls her eyes. Her mother finishes an old cross-stitch project while I order out for food. Later that day, Amy's ball takes out the six- and ten-pins. We awaken Katie and tell her it's her turn.

Her delivery is much like her sister's, but with a tad more oomph. Her ball starts left, hits the bumper designed to stop it from going into the gutter, veers back across the lane, hits the right bumper, then back across the lane to the left bumper, and so on and so forth, until it reaches the end of the lane and knocks down the ten-pin. She cheers for herself until she realizes she trails her younger sister two-to-one after one frame. She stomps off.

Debbie, who has never bowled, puts down her needlework, selects a pretty blue ball from the rack, takes a classic four-step approach, releases the ball and watches it zip down the lane, where it caroms off the right bumper before exploding into the pocket. When the dust clears, no pins are left standing. She turns and smiles. "Your turn, honey!" I say I'll just keep score.

Next time: "Invasion of the Miniature Golfers."

Responsibility Rears Its Ugly Head

It occurred to me yesterday while waiting in the drive-through at Burger King—my four-year-old seated at my side, dressed in red crinoline and satin because she had just had her picture made for an upcoming dance recital, me getting takeout instead of cooking because I had spent the afternoon shuttling my children from daycare to doctor to home to dance while my wife was lying on the couch with a sick stomach—that the last time I actually had control of my life was one day during the spring semester of my junior year in college.

I'm not complaining. It's just that if you think about it, it's amazing how much time you spend taking care of kids. Shortly after the birth of our first child, it became an ongoing conversation between my wife and me to wonder aloud what we did with our time before we became parents, fully responsible for the feeding, clothing, bathing, peace of mind and general welfare of a brand new human being.

Before kids, we actually used to sit around at night and ask what do you want to do, I don't know, what do you want to do?

It's the kind of thing that can keep you awake. If you sit down with a calculator and figure out you are spending more than a thousand dollars a year for diapers, it can get you down. Parents should avoid such depressing exercises. Besides, your child won't always be in diapers. If you can hang on for two or three years, you're home free. No more big expenses. Right?

While this line of reasoning is fundamentally flawed, it serves the purpose of preventing a grown man from turning into a mound of Jello and dripping through the cracks in the floor. Don't think about it and you'll be fine.

But I tend toward the world of reality, which sometimes rubs my wife the wrong way. Realistic people don't buy new cars, for example, because everyone knows new cars depreciate the moment you drive them off the lot. "It just doesn't make sense for us to get a new mini-van," I tell her, patiently explaining the realistic implications of such a purchase, to which she responds, "It also doesn't make sense to be mistaken for the Flintstones out for a night at the Bedrock Drive-In."

Such frank dialogue representing two independent philosophies is actually healthy for a family. Somewhere between our two extremes, we usually strike a balance. While our kids don't have a pair of Reeboks for each day of the week, they also don't have to put a flattened Prince Albert can in the soles of their shoes, which is what our grandparents had to do when they walked ten miles through the snow everyday, uphill both ways, just for the opportunity to sit in a frigid one-room school and do their work on a slate because they couldn't afford paper and pencil, thank you very much.

In addition to the expenses of food, clothing, dance lessons, day-care, allergy shots and bubblegum, I am reminded each day, because I work at a college, that in about four thousand days my first child will be starting college. A friend of mine who was trying to sell me an investment plan told me to think of it in terms of days instead of years, which he said really drives home the urgency. Now I have another reason not to be asleep at three in the morning. In order to have enough money to send both my children to college, I have calculated that I would have to save half of all my take-home pay for the next eleven years. Again, this is reality-thinking. Avoid it.

Besides the financial responsibilities that go along with raising children, there is the nagging fear that your daughter will someday roar off into the dusty sunset on the back of a motorcycle. Thoughts like these sneak up when you least expect them. You're dropping your four-year-old off at preschool when some scruffy little boy runs out to greet her and trips over his own shoelaces. You go weak, and you're no good for the rest of the day. This is when you wonder if your sense of responsibility will be enough to get you through the next eighteen years, after which time you won't have to worry because your kids will be grown. Right?

Sometimes it all weighs heavy, and I recall that day during my junior year in college when I felt I was in control of my own destiny. What if I had chosen to pack my bags and travel around the world? What if I had decided never to marry and have two kids and a mortgage and a neighbor dog that sits outside my back door with sad eyes until I give her a piece of beef jerky? What if I weren't going to see the little girl in the red crinoline dress graduate from three-year-old preschool this week?

I would be an empty man.

Children Surprise Us

Like a brave soldier, she marches through the door, head high, chin forward, ready to face whatever waits on the other side. If there is any doubt, her eyes do not betray her. The last thing I see is a cascade of brown hair falling nearly to her waist as the door closes behind her, shutting her off from her safe world of books and Barbies and gymnastics, locking her deep within a place of stainless steel, starched white uniforms and hypodermic needles.

For the few minutes she is gone, I try not to think about the fact that my six-year-old is getting another shot in the arm as part of a twice-weekly regimen the doctor prescribed to get her allergies under control. I am amazed at how gracefully she handles it. I was terrified as a kid when I had to get a shot. Even today, the thought of someone sliding a shiny pointed metallic object underneath my physical skin gives me a serious case of the heebie-jeebies.

Moments later, she returns and starts looking through the magazines stacked on the table in search of a Highlights she hasn't already read. No tears, no flushing, no evidence whatsoever that she has gone through anything more unpleasant than having her bangs curled. Again, I am amazed—and thankful. I am more confident with each visit that this isn't going to be as hard as I feared.

Children surprise. Whenever I think I'm in tune with one of these little people who live in my house, they say or do something unexpected, an electric bolt out of the clear blue sky, reminding me that, for all my vaulted grownup understanding, my children are in fact complex human beings with thoughts so deep and wide that no other person will ever completely understand them, certainly not I. The thought that their minds are more than miniature reproductions of their mother's and mine is exciting. There's something working inside them that's independent of either of us, and it is new everyday. I can't wait till tomorrow to see who my kids are.

One day I feel sure I know them; the next day I'm not so sure. We sometimes refer to Amy, our four-year-old, as the freight train, because she goes full tilt all the time. When we awaken her in the morning, she bounces up, ready to get on with the stuff of the day. Her wheels are in motion the moment she opens her eyes. All we have to do is put her down on the tracks, and she's off, nonstop, until she completes the day-long trip and arrives, spent, at the train station, her bed. She goes long and hard. She grabs play time by the scruff of the neck and drags it around until it faints from exhaustion. Her waking hours are all hers, and she will not be cheated. But at the end of the day, when the locomotive starts slowing, when the whippoorwill tunes up with the crickets for a twilight serenade, she rests her head on my shoulder and recalls the day's more interesting whistle-stops. Her stories are usually about who did what to whom and who said it was wrong and who brought some new stickers to Miss Lou's. Sometimes, though, from that rich mix of experiences, there suddenly blooms a child's insight. It can slip by unnoticed if I'm paying too much attention to the baseball game on TV. Before she falls asleep, she is reflective, and I love to hear her think out loud.

Even as Amy races through the day, Katie takes a slow, sweet walk. If something catches her eye, she stops to inspect it. She chooses carefully the things that matter to her, and she is patient with the time she devotes to them. She thinks before she acts. When we told her that allergy shots might help her, she asked logical, thoughtful questions. She talked to her friend Mandy, who also gets allergy shots, and came to the conclusion that it was probably the best thing. May as well get on with it. No big deal.

So now she just walks in and gets her shot, and that's it. And every time she does, I'm surprised.

May I Mistake Your Order?

I pulled into the drive-through and ordered with the air of one who has done this sort of thing before: "Three Chicken Tenders, please."

"Chicken Tenders?" the metal speaker questioned.

I detected confusion in the chicken person's voice, so I scanned the menu to see if Chicken Tenders were sold at this establishment. Nope—no Chicken Tenders to be had here. My brain, without my permission, decided I would stand my ground.

"Yes," I stammered, "three Chicken Tenders, or Chickenettes, or whatever you call those things."

"Three Chicken Littles. Will there be anything else, sir?"

I struggled to convey the rest of my order. "Yes. I'd like three two-piece dinners, extra crispy, all-white, substitute fries on ..."

"Two three-piece dinners and what, sir?"

"No, that's three two-piece dinners with—"

"Would you like fries with that?"

My wife slipped on a headscarf and sunglasses and pretended to study the comings and goings at the convenience store in the next parking lot. My own children, who have been known to be so uninhibited as to hang out of the car window and flag down strangers in grocery store parking lots, slumped in their seats.

The chicken attendant and I eventually hammered out a compromise, and I drove to the window. People in the restaurant watched us as we passed. They didn't even try hard to hide their amusement. They heard the whole thing over the loudspeaker and were waiting to see the dork who had ordered Chicken Tenders can you believe it?

It was embarrassing, but how many times had I sat in their place and giggled when someone who had serious doubts about whether the sound of his voice would obey the laws of physics and be transmitted through the speaker wire resorted to shouting his order? (Can I help you? YES! I'D LIKE A HAMBURGER AND FRIES, PLEASE! You don't have to shout, sir. OKAY, I WON'T!)

There's also the rubbernecker, the person who pulls up to the speaker and cranes his neck toward the speaker as though to greet the chicken person with a ceremonial kiss. And some rubberneck- ers are also shouters, on which occasion even the last person in line knows way too much about how they like their Whopper with extra pickles.

Some drive-throughs are not fully functional. There is one ham- burger place that won't respond when you drive up unless you step out of your car and jump on the air hose. Another place likes to startle you into a hearty appetite by turning up the volume on the speaker so it can cut through the roar of a 747. You drive up, and you wait—they let you sit for a few seconds to lull you to sleep—and suddenly the speaker explodes across your eardrum with the blunt force of a direct lightning strike, and the person on the other end says, "WELCOME TO LSOIUDJF, SOHNVIU DI ISJDL TIEIJOSK YHOIUR IWPODSDK?"

To which you respond, "Yes, I'd like three Chicken Tenders, please."

Someone's Thinking of Me

In the animated adventure, "An American Tail," Fievel and his stow- away family leave their homeland to voyage to America, a wonderful place where there are no cats, or so they have been told. (Fievel is a mouse.) At sea, a storm comes up, and a wall of water sweeps Fievel overboard. His family fears the worst. Heartbroken, they continue on to America. But Fievel's sister refuses to believe he has perished. Every night, before she falls asleep, she gazes across the harbor and sings to her brother. Fievel, who has miraculously survived the storm and is safe on shore, sings back across the darkness from somewhere just beyond her hearing. It is an aching duet:

> *Somewhere out there,*
> *Beneath the pale moonlight,*
> *Someone's thinking of me*
> *And loving me tonight.*
> *Somewhere out there,*
> *Someone's saying a prayer*
> *That we'll find one another*
> *In that big somewhere out there.*

Amy, our four-year-old, cries when she hears that song. I don't know if it's because of sadness for Fievel or because the melody is so beautiful. Perhaps it's both.

I do know she sometimes thinks about what it would be like to be separated from Mommy and Daddy. Once, in the drugstore, she ran away from me to explore. When she came back, I was not there. That night, before she went to sleep, she told me she'd been afraid I was lost. She held that scary thought in her head all day. Yesterday, Amy and I took her older sister to the doctor for an allergy shot. The girls stood behind me while I signed in at the window. Amy was distracted and didn't notice that we had walked away. She suddenly found herself standing with strangers, and I saw her eyes widen. She ran to me and buried her face on my shoulder.

But she is not a clingy child. If anything, she is too independent for her own good. Forcing her to hold my hand while crossing the parking lot requires warnings too many to count. And making sure she doesn't ride her bicycle in the road is like patrolling the Persian Gulf. Most of the time, she is as brave as her male compatriots. But there are other times, just before she falls asleep, when she allows me access to her thoughts, dreams and fears. She tells me the teddy bear on the wall looks like a monster when the light is turned off, so would I please move it?

Such fleeting glimpses into my children's thoughts come and go as quickly as a meteor streaking across a summer sky. The glimpses remind me of how lucky I am. I was thinking about this a few weeks ago when Debbie and I, leaving on a trip, kissed them goodbye and told them to be good. We were just a few miles down the road when Amy's song came to us over the radio ...

Somewhere out there,
Beneath the pale moonlight,
Someone's thinking of me
And loving me tonight.

Secret Trails

Yesterday afternoon we came home to discover that bulldozers had transformed the woods across the street into a dusty lot. There were only a few scraggly trees remaining along with some mounds of dirt here and there. Our daughters were elated. With a new place awaiting exploration, they dumped their book bags on the kitchen table and rushed to their bicycles. They pedaled furiously down the driveway and across the street, bumping along trails stamped into the dirt by the bulldozer's treads. After supper they beckoned us to come see their "secret trails."

Maybe there is something about freshly turned soil that ignites a sense of expectancy—a genetic trigger announcing the earth's readiness to grow seed into life-sustaining food.

Then again, maybe it's just fun to ride your bike in the dirt. I've heard other parents say that no matter how many toys their children have, they quickly become bored and seek new stimulation. Amy has a Barbie Ferrari to transport her collection of Barbie-people, but she would just as soon use an old shoe of mine to chauffeur Barbie around the metropolis that is our den floor. And although Katie has a room of her own, she likes to go into her closet and arrange it to suit her tastes. Her closet is her retreat, a place to read or color or listen to New Kids on the Block.

I'm always surprised by their imagination. The other day my wife called me to the window. I looked out and saw the two of them, in bathing suits, sharing the same swing, the younger in her sister's lap, pointing a hose straight up into the air and laughing as the water splashed down on them.

Where does this imagination come from, and where can I get some? I used to have it. As a boy I played army with sticks and pine cones. I pressed bottle caps into the bank of a gully and pretended I was at the controls of a submarine. Sometimes my closet was a Mercury space capsule. My cousin Gary and I played on a hammock that transformed into a life raft surrounded by sharks that would bite off our legs if we dropped them over the side, which we did repeatedly.

It is fun to give in to imagination, but at some point rude reality elbows its way to the front. We learn that studying leads to good grades, which leads to a good job, which leads to a good house, which leads to good clothes for your kids. And on it goes. Nowhere in the formula does it say you're supposed to have fun doing this reality stuff.

That's about the time my child nearly pulls the backdoor off the hinges as she bursts into the kitchen, grabs my hand and drags me out the door to see her secret trails. She pedals gleefully over a mound of dirt, and I kick a few clods around and think to myself, wouldn't this be a great place to play army?

Stuck in the Middle

Help. The giant vacuum cleaner of life is sucking me into the dust bag of middle age.

It all started innocently enough—a sore muscle here, a little less hair there. Then one night while watching the Tonight Show with Jay Leno, I found myself missing Johnny Carson ... and Doc and Ed ... and Karnac the Magnificent. Then, because I am getting older, I nodded off.

My children, who go out of their way to convince other people they are angels, began tossing the word "dork" in my direction. "Daddy!" they howled, looking through my high school yearbook, "were you always a dork?"

I have crossed The Great Divide. The signs are there:

I feel uncomfortable if I'm not home before dark.

I think about my yard a lot. A lot.

My dog and I are about the same age in dog years, and all she does is lie around and scratch.

I feel compelled to defend Barry Manilow songs.

I am consumed with the knowledge that as I age my body will begin to consume the calcium in my bones. I will literally become a cannibal.

My idea of a romantic night with my wife is supper at Mama Penn's and a stock-up run to Walmart.

I appreciate people who listen respectfully when I brag about how long my Snapper can go between belt changes, and I watch too much of the Discovery Channel.

I've reached an awkward stage of life. When you're in your twenties and thirties, young folks seem to like being around you. (By the way, "young folks" is a term you start using when you hit middle age.) You're still one of them, only a more mature, cooler version. Likewise, when you hit seventy or so, they think you're cool because you can be a crotchety old man and get away with it. But I am not seventy. I am in the middle. The middle is boring. The middle gets no respect.

I've inherited the forsaken minivan my wife once insisted she had to have. She, on the other hand, has a flip-phone and drives a sporty car with alloy wheels. It's hard to be taken seriously as a happening dude—and only a dork would say "happening dude"—when you pull into a parking lot full of happening college students and you are behind the wheel of an unhappening aged minivan with peeling imitation woodgrain siding. As I walk past them, the students ignore me. I am forty. I am irrelevant.

I sometimes want to throw a pity party for myself when I think of the things I'll never do. I'll never play major league baseball or be an astronaut. I'll never ride a bicycle across the country with only a sleeping bag and a camera on my back.

But it's okay. I've enjoyed a few things in my four decades on this planet. I've seen a man walk on the moon, watched Hank Aaron hit his 715th home run and witnessed my children's births. I played guitar in a teenage rock-and-roll band, and I've fished with my dad. I bought a house, several vehicles and a dog. I built my own deck and a treehouse for my kids. I married one fine-looking woman, and I've single-handedly driven one previously owned minivan almost 100,000 miles.

Flush with the insightful maturity that comes with these

achievements, I was on the verge of understanding the Meaning of Life. Then Ed McMahon said the Meaning of Life had been hermetically sealed and kept in a mayonnaise jar under Funk and Wagnalls' porch since noon today.

Where is the great Karnac when I need him most?

A Dog's Life

My name is Millie, and I lead a dog's life (due to the fact that I am a dog, but please don't tell my human family because they don't know).

I spend most of the day sleeping. The rest of the time I devote to my hobbies: barking menacingly at walkers while also wagging my tail, scratching, ignoring my Purina Dog Chow, scratching, dragging home dead animals, scratching, and breathing on people until they lose consciousness (but not necessarily in that order—sometimes I scratch first).

As a golden retriever, my favorite activity that doesn't involve scratching is retrieving things. My master calls it petty theft. I especially enjoy bringing home a single solitary shoe—never a matching pair—from any unguarded carport in our neighborhood. I don't chew on the shoe, I just like having it around. Humans sleep with teddy bears, I sleep with an old shoe. Don't judge.

The biggest item I ever retrieved was a window frame. The problem was that the window frame was attached to my master's house.

One day I brought home a dead beaver. I found him, he was dead, so I dragged him home. (I'm a retriever—what can I say?) Other items I've retrieved over the years: a freshly grilled T-bone steak, a bag of powdered doughnuts, numerous small animals (deceased and semi-deceased), a head of cabbage, an unopened container of Jello pudding and assorted articles of clothing.

I like to think of myself as a discriminating retriever. Never, for instance, have I retrieved a common stick. There are, of course, dogs who enjoy this sort of thing. The wacky dog who lives next door loves to retrieve rocks. His name is Wolfie, and he thoroughly enjoys barking like a Looney Tune directly at the ground, for he has figured out that's where rocks live. A human person can throw a rock, and Wolfie will calculate its flight path, run like a maniac to the exact spot where the rock will fall from the sky, and catch it in his teeth. This pooch is a ballistics genius, but he catches rocks with his teeth. He is a dog biscuit shy of a full box.

When I'm not retrieving, I spend a lot of time thinking about dog stuff: What are the social implications of tail-wagging? How is it that three-day-old potato peels taste better than Purina Dog Chow? Is this the day the garbage truck comes? If a tree falls in a forest and no one is there to hear it, will it kill a beaver? Can Wolfie actually smell the rock in the creek when he puts his nose under the water and inhales?

Ultimately, my eyelids grow heavy, and sleep warms me like a comfortable blanket, and all my questions distill into one eternal doggie dilemma:

To scratch or not to scratch? That is the question.

Women Are from Venus
(Which Explains a Lot)

My wife, an intense person even on a normal day, has gone on a diet. The stress-o-meter at our house has come off its hinges. My dog quit sleeping on the porch and is bedding down at the edge of the woods.

I should point out that my wife doesn't need to go on a diet. And I don't say that just because it's recommended in the bestseller, Women Are from Venus, Men Are from Way Out Yonder Somewhere Altogether Different. She looks great. I don't think she needs to go on a diet, but she believes she does, and I've learned after almost fourteen years of marriage that when she's convinced of something … well, there you go.

When a woman is thinking dark thoughts about how she looks, a negative chain reaction ensues. She sees everything as part of a conspiracy. Laundry that only the day before was merely a pile of dirty clothes suddenly is demon-possessed. Its sole devil purpose is to multiply when she leaves the room. Same thing with dishes and dirty kitchen floors. ("Tell me you did not walk on that floor I just swept.") The husband-father appliance, who says, "It's just laundry, honey," is a clueless bag of tell-me-you-did-not-just-say-that. Children transmute into adrenaline-charged little human dump trucks, randomly depositing their possessions hither and yon across the freshly swept floor.

Women view dieting differently than men, who consider losing weight, like anything else, a challenge—a mountain to be climbed, a number to be circled on the score card, an opportunity to prove we can still WIN! For a woman to admit she needs to lose weight— correct me if I'm wrong here—is the end of the world. A guy says, "I need to work off this spare tire." A woman will stand in front of a mirror and say to her reflection, "You are a cow."

(It is here, men—and I can't stress this enough—that you must dig deep for an appropriately sensitive response. "Honey, you don't look like a cow" is barely adequate. However, "The most beautiful of all the angels in heaven would trade her wings to have a figure like yours" is a decent start. To be safe, don't compare her figure to that of any farm animal.)

Before my wife signed up for the diet/fitness program, she de- cided to work out with a Jane Fonda exercise video. I was brushing my teeth, which is the extent of my physical fitness routine, when I heard pounding music and Jane barking out encouragement in the next room (cha-boom, cha-boom, "Streeeetch!" cha-boom, cha- boom, "Streeeetch!"). It was then that my wife was waylaid by the Mutant Alien Leg Cramp from Beyond the Solar System. She was seriously hurting, and it was not at all funny, except when she cried, "Rub it DON'T RUB IT Rub it DON'T RUB IT!" That part was sort of funny. Our daughters were witnesses. Katie was trying very hard not to laugh. Amy believed her mother to be seriously injured and began weeping like a faulty Price-Pfister faucet. Our house is a very, very, very fine house.

It was a rough beginning, but things are running smoothly again. My wife drinks a lot of water and says she feels good, and her power-walking is becoming the stuff of legend. She is almost at her target weight, and I've no doubt she'll reach it. She's unrelenting.

Not that she needed to lose the weight, mind you. She looked great before she started all this. Now she looks great … even more … with less.

I'm stopping now.

Lone Ranger

I live with three women, a female golden retriever and six hermit crabs of indeterminate gender. Woe unto me.

Don't get me wrong. Some of my best friends are women. My mother is a woman, and so were both my grandmothers. I come from a long line of female ancestors who were women.

Being the only male in a house full of females does have its redeeming qualities—bathrooms, for example. I've staked my claim to the "guest" bathroom and instructed my daughters to keep their beauty products in the other bathroom with their mother's stuff. Why do a ten- and an almost-thirteen-year-old need beauty products, anyway? Katie, our older daughter, insists on covering her perfectly smooth face with powder—"to make it smoother." I don't like this, and I am not hesitant to say so in an authoritative tone, at which point she applies more smoothing powder to her smooth face, and I walk away wondering when I became background noise. She has her mother's permission to use makeup. Because she answers to a higher authority, she can ignore me.

Amy, not to be outdone, is experimenting with creative techniques for applying hairspray. Instead of directing the hairspray onto her hair, which seems to me a sensible approach, she sprays beauty product into the air for about fifteen seconds and then walks in circles trying to the get the airborne TRESemme molecules to bond with her bangs. Apparently this practice is good for the hair, but also for the carpet, which has taken on the consistency of Astroturf.

My wife, whom I would not wish to offend by leaving her out, has her own morning beauty ritual. I know when it's time for me to get out of bed simply by listening to the running of her hairdryer. If it runs without interruption, I can roll over and sleep for another twenty minutes. But if I hear the hairdryer start, then stop, then drop to the countertop ... start, stop, CLUNK ... start, stop, CLUNK ... I know she is putting the final touches on her coiffure and it's almost time for Bryant and Katie and the Today show. So long, Mr. Pillow; hello, Willard Scott.

There are other interesting dynamics in a household where you're outnumbered three to one—movies, for instance. Will we see Macho Guy Takes Out Evil Dictator and His Heavily Armed Thugs with Only a Swiss Army Knife or Latest Disney Project to Shamelessly Attract Kids Who Bring Along Their Parents and Their Wallets? Or, on TV, will we watch reruns of Andy Griffith or Ice Dancing Exponanza?

There are other advantages to being the only male in a house full of women. To whom else will they go to ask, "Which earring looks better with this outfit?" or, "Daddy, can you tie my hair ribbon?" or, "Can I have five dollars for lunch money?" Who but I will build shelves to hold their collection of Babysitter Club books? Who will take them on hikes in the woods or explain to them the variety of crabgrasses in our yard?

Another advantage to being the only man in the house is that I get random hugs and kisses. Sometimes I'll be sitting on the couch, expertly operating my remote control, when this happens.

Mine is a tough job, but somebody has to do it.

Utopia-by-the-Sea

Utopia. The dictionary describes it as an "ideally perfect place."

For one week every summer, our family lives in Utopia. It's a magical place where the ocean calls to you from the backyard to come out and play.

It's a place where you can watch your kids shovel frantically to build a wall of sand against the incoming tide. They fully believe they can stop the ocean, and, for a hopeful moment, you believe it, too.

It's people in bathing suits—all shapes, sizes, shades and styles: middle-aged women with leathery skin roasted to a deep brown; muscular teenage boys with their baseball caps on backwards, tossing a football and diving after it headfirst into the surf; teenage girls in myriad hues of neon bikinis; an overweight woman with bleached hair, sitting in a low-slung chair in the surf, smoking cigarettes and sipping something from her cooler; people lying on towels every-where, soaking up cancer rays, satisfied in their conclusion that the payoff is worth the risk; a pretty young woman walking by, her shoulders slumped because she is painfully conscious of her own appearance; a fifty-ish man sporting a generous tummy and Italian-style bikini briefs (there ought to be a law).

It's old people bending over to inspect every shell they see. It's Jet Skis bounding across the whitecaps, guided by testosterone-powered young men. It's airplanes towing advertising banners for restaurants and tee-shirt shops. It's a kid pushing a rolling lemonade stand up and down the beach, working for minimum wage and tips. It's fathers lifting squealing toddlers by the hands and dipping them in the surf while mothers take pictures.

It's evenings spent walking along the beach, perhaps all the way to the pier, where bevies of teenage girls roam the boardwalk, first to one end and then the other, giggling at boys clustered along the edges. Sullen young men stare back boldly—something they would never do back home. Crusty old men cast fishing lines into the black swells, oblivious to the hum and crackle of adolescent energy all around them. At the end of the pier, a country music band bangs out one tune after another as happy vacationers lose their inhibitions and join a line dance.

It's miniature golf, roller coasters, water rides and boogie boards.

It's fun.

But it's more.

It's a place where jobs, responsibilities, laundry and unmown lawns cease to exist. It's a place where you trade in your laptop computer for a paperback novel. It's a place where your biggest decision is whether or not to go back for a third helping at the seafood buffet.

It's cool breezes and lazy afternoons. It's people smiling and laughing. It's a place where you can take a nap whenever you feel like it.

It's an escape.

The first thing you see after driving five hours to get there is a plaque mounted on the front of the house:

Dedicated to
Leonard A. Muth
1921-1971
Whose dreams and
hard work made this
house a Utopia in 1953.
1954—Hurricane Hazel
1989—Hurricane Hugo

Even in the dead of winter, when a cold wind cuts through the barren trees in my backyard, I can close my eyes, and I'm on the porch of the Muth House, sitting in a rocking chair with my feet propped up, watching children chase minnows in the surf.

It's nice to know not even a hurricane can take that away.

Katie Turns Thirteen

Our family train is pulling into Adolescence Junction. Katie, our oldest, just turned thirteen. From what I can surmise from my vast parental knowledge, the next few years can go either of two ways: (one) uneventfully, or (two) like a wicked runaway hormone roller coaster at the Amusement Park from Neptune.

When I tell my coworkers our daughter has become a teenager, they pat me on the back and walk away, shaking their heads.

"What?!" I call after them.

"You'll see," they say. "Oh, yes, you'll definitely see." Then they turn and walk away again.

"What?!"

I shared this experience with my pastor, a learned man and author of the popular golfer's adage, "Boys, it just doesn't get any better than this." I was hoping for a golden nugget of wisdom. He instead offered a chunk of coal: "Better you than me." This from a man only now emerging from the long dark tunnel of teenager parenthood, himself. My confidence in the Old Wise One was shaken. If his was a rough ride, what pitfalls await me?

I don't see what all the gloom is about. Katie is a pleasant person, and I can't imagine this happy little cheerleader suddenly transforming into a venom-spewing space alien.

To be honest, there are times when she's not exactly super-nice … like when I try to wake her up in the morning and she flings herself all the way to the far side of the bed and hisses, "Don't DO that!" But she gets it honest—I'm not a morning person, either. Also, sometimes, after you tell her for the fifth time to brush her teeth, she might slam her fist into the couch, stand up with a flourish, cast a withering look at you and stomp majestically out of the room. (I would say she gets this trait from her mother, but I don't need another withering glance directed my way.)

But this is pretty routine stuff, and I don't see any storm clouds gathering on the horizon. My teenager still likes to spend time with her dad. We've discovered fishing. She baits her own hook and everything. She also likes to sit beside me on the couch and watch whatever I want to watch. She likes to shoot baskets. She still wants a goodnight kiss.

So far, adolescence hasn't shown its ugly side. But something else has: hairy-legged boys. This definitely is not cool. Someday she'll be going out with one of those boys, and I'll have to go fishing alone.

The calendar tells me she's thirteen, but my heart tells me it cannot be so. Kids change too fast. The early changes—crawling, walking and talking—were a lot more entertaining. Now the changes are more subtle, but they signify a profound truth: She will leave us someday.

Then things will have come full circle. She used to stand at the door every morning, barely tall enough to stretch up on tiptoe and watch through the window as I drove off to work. Someday, not too many years from now, she will drive away, and I will be the one standing at the door, watching.

We Love to Fly (And It Shows)

I allowed my children to fly on an airplane a few weeks ago. I did so after hearing protests every time I went on a trip and didn't take them along. Apparently, never having flown on a plane is about as humiliating as having your parents drop you off at school in a station wagon.

It's been years since I drove my kids to school in a station wagon. Ours was a handsome automobile—a long, blue-and-imitation-woodgrain-siding behemoth. Picture Clark Griswold's metallic-pea Wagon Queen Family Truckster in the original Family Vacation movie ... now imagine it spray-painted blue. Ours was one of the few family vehicles that came standard with eastern and western time zones. We could put the kids in the back seat and forget about them. Any disputes fell outside our range of hearing. They could elbow each other senseless back there and we'd never know. This feature alone made the car worth the purchase price.

Our family station wagon bore a noble name: the Oldsmobile Delta 88 Custom Cruiser. I've always liked the word "cruiser," because it implies power to spare. (Ladies and gentlemen, we're leveling off at our cruising altitude of 30,000 feet ... this is Captain James T. Kirk of the cruiser-class starship Enterprise ...) Our station wagon was a vehicle worthy of the name cruiser. It might not have been explosive off the starting line, but given a long enough runway, the 350-cubic-inch V-8 under the hood of this monster could eventually propel it to liftoff velocity. Put wings on it and you'd have had a woodgrain-paneled Space Shuttle.

Which brings us back to the subject of flying. To say our kids were excited when we told them they would be passengers on a jet plane would be an understatement. They bounced around like chihuahuas on performance-enhancing drugs. This reaction, of course, was in conspicuous contrast to the indifference our older daughter feigned when she casually mentioned the trip to a friend. "Yeah, I think we're flying, but I'm not sure," Katie said. (Shrug, disinterested sigh.)

No such pretense for Amy, the ten-year-old, who adopted the slogan, "I love to fly, and it shows. Seriously. It really shows." She eagerly shared with anyone, total strangers notwithstanding, that she was going to ride on an airplane and fold down a tray in front of her and people in uniforms would give her peanuts. To her, the anticipation of high-altitude dining far outshone the sobering prospect of hurtling through the atmosphere at 500 miles per hour, six miles above the earth. A personal fold-down tray and free peanuts ranked right up there with Christmas.

The excitement reached a fever pitch on the morning of the Big Day. The girls crammed enough stuff in their carry-on bags to stage an assault on a small republic. They were taught to pack that way by their mother, who wants to be prepared "just in case they lose our luggage." I've always winked and indulged her this insecurity, confident in knowing that the airlines have never lost my luggage.

We walked down the boarding chute, which was almost a religious experience for Amy, stepped onto the plane and found our seats. The girls immediately buckled their seat belts, then sat perfectly erect—heads pressed backward against their seats, eyes wide and straight ahead, fingers gripping armrests—and waited for takeoff.

After a few of minutes of taxiing, Amy leaned across the aisle and whispered, with some disappointment, "Is this it?" A moment later, we rushed down the runway, and the big aluminum bird nosed upward. Our daughters' expressions of apprehension turned to unbridled delight. I savored their moment and wished for a camera.

Within five minutes they were seasoned travelers. They lowered their trays, played cards and waited patiently for their peanuts and Cokes. They were cool. The Kodak Moment had passed, never to return.

It was a nice trip, except that on the way home the airline lost our luggage. I'm looking for an extra toothbrush. I would ask my wife, but she would enjoy it way too much.

Our Family Gets a Mailbox

We have something new beside the driveway: a mailbox. Not only is it a new mailbox, it is also our first mailbox. After fourteen years of marriage and eight years of living at the same address, I finally felt we were ready to welcome this iconic American object into our lives.

If you think about it, a mailbox is a major life commitment. It means you have decided to settle down for an extended stay. It also means you have decided to let everyone—and I do mean everyone—know where you live. I've always considered my home my private castle, and I can't imagine that King Arthur would have had a mailbox with "1 Camelot Moat" stenciled on the side. For most of our marriage, we have maintained a post office box a few miles from where we lived.

But one day I woke up and decided our family needed a mailbox, and I could hardly wait to drive to the hardware store to get one. I spent an hour studying the available selections, careful to choose the right model for our yard. Finally, satisfied in my choice of a cedar post with matching cedar-covered mailbox, I drove home and surprised the family. It was a special moment when the children met their new mailbox.

"What is it, Daddy?" asked the youngest, wonderstruck.

"It's called a mailbox, honey," I said, my voice quavering with pride.

"Why have we never had one before?" asked the oldest.

"Never mind that," I said.

The next afternoon, we gathered in a circle for the groundbreaking ceremony. My wife, who always knows just what to say at such occasions, said, "Be careful you don't puncture the water line, honey."

It must have been a strange sight—this group of three solemn watchers and an out-of-shape man trying to pound a hole through sun-baked clay. Motorists slowed and turned on their headlights, apparently possessed of the notion that we were burying a beloved pet. Anyone who has ever taken up post-hole diggers knows how difficult it is to hit the hole in the middle every time. The harder you pound the earth, the worse your aim. It is even harder to do if you start giggling, which we all did. The episode was instigated by my wife, who is known widely as a compulsive giggler. (She usually falls victim to the giggles at the dinner table when I am trying to effect a stern fatherly tone with my children. It's hard to discipline your kids for playing see-food when their mother is covering her eyes and struggling to keep from making a sound like SCHNOCKK! and spewing her mashed potatoes across the table.)

The giggles notwithstanding, I finally finished digging the hole. It was just the right depth. I know this because I measured it with my premium-gauge handyman tape-measure. I put the post in the ground, added concrete mix and skillfully leveled the post using a plumb line, which I made sure my family saw me using expertly.

"What is it?" my youngest asked. As I began to explain in easy-to-understand terms the beautiful simplicity of a plumb line, she yawned and asked if she could ride her bike.

I calibrated furiously for the next hour—eyeing, measuring, adjusting and readjusting—intent on having the subdivision's most perfectly plumb mailbox post.

The following morning, I awoke to find that my post was not plumb. But that's okay—once we attached the mailbox and planted a flower bed at the base, you could hardly tell. Mission accomplished.

My youngest then noticed the red flag on the side of the mailbox. "What is it?" she asked. I explained that she could write a letter to a friend, put it in the mailbox and raise the flag, and a mail-person would come and pick up her letter and deliver it to her friend.

"That is way cool," she said and rode away on her bike.

I went off to share this touching exchange with my wife, but she was eating mashed potatoes, so I just kept walking.

Confession of a Middle-Aged Mouseketeer

The largest family entertainment company in the history of the world was founded on a rodent. Millions of children have fallen victim to the charms of Mickey Mouse. I challenge you to find a child over the age of three who hasn't obtained his own personal copy of a Disney video, asked his parents to take him to Disney World, or belted forth with gusto the name of the leader of the band that's made for you and me: M-I-C-K-E-Y, M-O-U-S-E!

Children love Mickey Mouse, which makes it all the harder for me to say this out loud, but I must: I vacuumed up a baby mouse, and I did it on purpose.

An explanation is in order. We have a situation with mice in our garage. They like the garage because warm automobile engines offer cozy quarters on a winter night. Also, our dog Millie's food bowl provides a steady supply of high-protein supper nuggets. In short, our garage is a five-star Mouse Marriott.

On occasion, I have gone out to the garage after dark to check the oil, only to lift the hood and watch mice scatter in a well-rehearsed random pattern. Left behind on my engine block are acorn shells, half-gnawed Purina Dog Chow pieces and other telltale evidence, if you know what I mean.

At first I thought it was cute, until the mice decided that loitering under the hood wasn't enough. I first became aware of a deteriorating situation when I took my wife's car to Oil-R-Us, whose motto is "We smear only the finest synthetic grease on your driver's seat." The Automotive Lubrication Technician removed my air filter, did a double-take, then called me over for a consultation. Specifically, his question was: "Mr. Brum, why is there approximately one quart of Purina Dog Chow in your air breather unit?"

"DOG CHOW IN BAY ONE!" yelled someone from under my car.

All of the professional Automotive Lubrication Technicians thought this was very funny. "Mr. Broom, do you have a dog?" snickered the manager. "Should we remove this, or do you want to leave it in there?"

I looked at him with my "Really?" expression. "Just suck it up with the vacuum," I answered.

"VACUUMING DOG CHOW IN BAY ONE!"

The final straw came one night a couple of weeks ago when I opened the trunk of the car and saw bits of chewed paper. I emptied the trunk and began vacuuming up the mess. When I lifted the spare tire, there she was—Momma Mouse and her squeaky little offspring staring back with beady little eyes. I reacted on instinct. As they scurried in every direction, I jabbed blindly with the vacuum nozzle. THOOMP!

I realize this means my membership in the Mickey Mouse Club

will be revoked. Between you and me, I always liked Donald Duck better anyway.

Hairy-Legged Boys

It's 1997, which means we are passing some significant mileposts at our house: My youngest daughter just turned eleven, my friend is preparing for his daughter's wedding, and my dog and I are both middle-aged.

First, my growing child. With every new year comes another birthday for Amy, who decided to be born eleven years ago on January 6, 1986, the coldest morning in the history of the world. She chose this day so as not to be outdone by her older sister, who was born on the hottest afternoon in the history of the world: July 16, 1983. Eleven is a significant birthday because it marks the first time in her life she needs more than two hands to tell people how old she is. Eleven is an age when she's not a little kid anymore, but she's also not a big kid. She enjoys the benefits of both worlds. Eleven is also her first twin-digit birthday, and every succeeding twin-digit birthday (twenty-two, thirty-three, etc.) will occur once every eleven years. All of which makes eleven a pretty special birthday. On her next twin-digit birthday, she'll be twenty-two—a grown woman— which brings us to my next worry.

I've a friend, Bob, who is my age. Bob's twenty-two-year-old daughter is getting married this summer. I cannot imagine being old

enough to have a child who is planning to marry another person, especially if the other person is a hairy-legged boy who communicates
with shrugs and grunts. Not that Bob's future son-in-law is a woolly
monosyllabic, necessarily. I don't know that for sure.

Bob, an accountant by training and a professional athlete in
his dreams, has known his daughter's betrothed since the boy was
five. The kid used to dribble over with his basketball and ask Bob to
come out and play. This pleased Bob, who relished the opportunity
to teach the boy (the son he never had, blah, blah, blah) how to play
the game. When Bob's daughter turned seventeen, the hairy-legged
boy continued to come over but no longer asked Bob to come out
and play. Dumped Bob like last year's Air Jordans.

Speaking of old shoes, we now move to our third and final point
of anxiety, which involves Millie, my trusted golden-retriever-of-
neighbors'-shoes-left-unguarded-in-carports. In 1997, I will turn
forty-two. Millie will be the same age in dog years. (I, in dog years,
will be 294.)

My dog and I are both entering middle age together, and we
have a lot in common. We've both had our shots. We both enjoy
scratching, and we both have been known to consume other people's
uneaten food. She likes to roll around in the grass—I roll around on
the couch in search of the remote control. She's become more toler-
ant of other dogs that wander near our yard—I've learned to put up
with the boys who phone my daughters. Sometimes she'll pout if she
doesn't get enough attention—I've been accused of the same. We're
both getting a little droopy around the eyelids.

Her bark is worse than her bite, but I wouldn't want any hairy-legged boys to get the mistaken idea I've slipped that far.

View from a Banana Seat

The ten-speed bicycle I bought after we got married has hung upside-down from the rafters of our garage for a long time. I put it up there to get it out of the way. My wife's three-speed hangs beside mine, completing a sad picture. Our bikes are relics from our youth.

The kids' bikes are in the garage, too—tiny ones with wobbly training wheels, a shiny grownup-sized model Amy bought with her birthday money last year, plus all the other sizes in between. I've never thrown away any of their old bikes. Instead, I hang them from the rafters like artifacts on display at the Smithsonian.

My kids like to ride their bikes in our neighbors' driveways and in the street beside our house. I never let them out of my sight. When I was their age, my friends and I rode wherever we wanted and were gone all day. Our parents never worried about us, at least as far as we knew. Our summer days were spent taking in the countryside from the vantage point of a banana seat. We knew every inch of backroad and dirt road within five miles of our subdivision. If there was a good fishing bridge, we could be at it when the fish were biting. We kept a running inventory of the best roadside trash dumps. We knew exactly where the deepest tar spots were, where we slammed on brakes to squeal our tires and made them smoke.

We popped wheelies and staged drag races. Sometimes we wiped out and put Mercurochrome on our injuries. We took turns jumping over ramps and each other, and we blazed trails through the woods. We ran over live snakes and dead frogs, kicked at barking dogs at full pedal, and taped walkie-talkies to the handlebars and pretended to be policemen. We delivered GRIT newspapers to our neighbors, and we clothes-pinned baseball cards to the spokes so that our bikes sounded like motorcycles. We repaired our own flats with the Patch-a-Leak tins we carried in our pockets, and we dragged the toes of our Converse Chuck Taylors along the road surface until the rubber wore through. We parked our bikes in a circle, our front tires pointing toward the center, and we talked … about baseball, about fishing, about bikes.

I wish my children could experience bicycle years like mine. If I were to let them pedal over the hill, they would probably be fine. But probably isn't good enough. I can't cut them loose with the same freedom I enjoyed, but I can ride with them. I bought new tubes and tires for my bike last week, and I intend to oil the chain and hit the open road next chance I get.

The Time that Binds

As if parents don't have enough guilt, we now learn that spending quality time with our children isn't as important as we once thought for raising well-adjusted young adults. According to a recent Newsweek article, researchers are beginning to agree that the amount of time you spend with your kids is more important than what you do when you're with them.

"Kids don't do meetings," the writer scolds. "You can't raise them in short, scheduled bursts. They need lots of attention, and experts warn that working parents may be shortchanging them."

You know what this means, of course. It means that when my wife reads this, I'll be banned from the Atlanta Braves for a month. "Instead of watching adult millionaires play a children's game on television," she'll say with one eyebrow arched, "why don't you go outside and play baseball with your children?"

To which I, master of disarming wit, will reply, "Oh, yeah?"

She's right. I should be spending more time with my kids.

There. I feel better.

I lied. I feel guilty. Fathers should spend more time with their children, but it's quicker said than done. You rationalize, telling yourself you work too many hours, schedules are too full and life is too hectic. But you don't do anything about it. You whine, and then you get up the next morning and do the same thing all over again.

Then you come home from work one day and your children are budding young adults with interests of their own, and they may not want to play baseball with you anymore.

Another point in the Newsweek article was this: Even though fathers are performing somewhat better than they were twenty years ago, mothers still do the majority of work related to raising children.

Ouch.

Sometimes I'll wash the dishes or push the vacuum cleaner around, and I'll walk around feeling pretty good about myself.
But it's my wife who handles most of the child-rearing duties at our
house: getting the girls up and ready for school, chauffeuring, helping with homework, talking with teachers, buying clothes and shoes,
doing laundry, helping with school fundraisers, offering construc-
tive commentary on cheering or gymnastics routines, or listening to
their problems.

I like to think of this as a great partnership in which my wife and
I bring our separate but equal skills to raising our children. Her job is
to produce intelligent, healthy, emotionally balanced female persons.
My job is to be there when they stand on one leg and ask, "Daddy,
which shoe goes better with this outfit?"

To which I respond, "That one."

At which point they go with the other one, the one their mom
likes.

Aliens Among Us

The spaceship lurking behind the Hale-Bopp Comet has snuck down
and deposited two aliens at my house.

The larger one is from planet Cheer. I think she is queen of her
planet, because she calls herself "Cheer Leader." From all outward
appearances, this alien could pass for a human adolescent—she
wears an orthodontic retainer at night, exhibits selective hearing loss

and rolls her eyes because she is always misunderstood. She looks normal enough, but so does alien number two.

The smaller alien is from an uncharted corner of the galaxy. She calls herself Gymnast. Ask her age, and she says, "Eleven revolutions around the puny star you call Sun," at which point she attempts a back walkover, knocking over a lamp and bounding out of the room in her frenzied alien locomotion.

I think it is clear what has happened: The Hale-Bopp spaceship has abducted my daughters and left two impostors behind. In talking with other parents, I have learned that finding one's children have been swapped for aliens is not unusual. "Weirdest thing," a friend said. "We went to bed one night and little Johnny was fine. The next morning he was an alien. The space people finally brought back the real Johnny when he was twenty-eight ... just when I was starting to bond with Alien Johnny."

But back to my own space invaders. While they look normal, they exhibit other-worldly behavior. The one who calls herself Cheer Leader walks around the house flailing her limbs. Upon closer inspection, I discover there is a pattern to her flailing. Her movements are not random at all, but carefully choreographed jerks, hiccups, kicks, lunges and spasms. I believe these are part of an elaborate signaling language she uses to communicate with her "people."

Cheer Leader speaks in a perky manner. While practicing her flailing, she yells in a cadence that is first down, then UP, then down, then back UP. She says things like, "Let's GO big RED!" or "All RIGHT mus-TANGS!" She does this at inappropriate times, like at the dinner table: "Please PASS the jell-LEE!" or, when directed at her alien sister: "Pul-LEASE shut UP!"

"I think not, spunky sister unit," says the alien called Gymnast, executing a textbook roundoff and kicking a box of Pop Tarts across the kitchen.

Gymnast's planet, it would seem, is a place where the inhabitants are incapable of moving from one spot to another using only their legs. Instead, they get around by means of cartwheels, backflips and assorted gyrations. Gymnast cannot go from one room to another without imitating a back-breaking movement named after a petite Russian person.

I sometimes sit on my couch, nursing the remote control, when I hear Gymnast cartwheeling down the hallway: thump-thump-thump (pause), thump-thump-thump (pause). One day after the thump-thump-thump (pause), I heard thump-THUMP! OWWW! Miss Gymnast, meet Mr. Wall. Beam me up, Scottie.

Doctor of Laughter

Laughter is good for us. It exercises the cardiovascular system and burns calories. A belly laugh can stretch seldom-used muscles, including those in the face, which can make us look younger. In addition, laughter triggers our bodies to release chemicals that make us feel better.

There's nothing bad about laughing, unless you're in a situation where laughing is inappropriate—like in a church service. The temptation to giggle is most powerful there. I've seen a pew almost shake apart from the forces of stifled laughter.

My daughter, who laughs like a hyena on nitrous oxide, doesn't waste much time in the giggle stage. Katie, fourteen, is a petite young thing with a reserved public demeanor. But tell her a funny story or dribble gravy on your shirt, or stumble on a word while trying to place an order at the drive-through window, and she lapses into a fit—an uncontrollable, fall-down-on-the-floor, hysterical laughing fit.

Just say the word "guffaw." That alone is enough to set her off. "Guf-(snicker)-faw," she repeats, folding up and falling down in a giggle spasm. "GUFFAW!" In short order, howling and ... well, guffawing, ensue. Another word that sets her off is "schnock," a term I invented to describe the sound my wife makes when she herself gets caught up in an extended giggle. (Usage: "Stop schnocking and eat your mashed potatoes.")

These bouts of laughter can occur anywhere, but the best ones happen at home, where Katie feels free to let it all out. Many a family dinner has degenerated into an out-of-control group guffaw. The volume this small person can generate is astounding. She doesn't just laugh—she howls. Serious wheezing and belly-clutching are involved. She goes weak in the knees. She hyperventilates. She curls up on the floor and bangs her feet on the carpet.

Her laughter is contagious. Once it starts, everything is funny. Almost as enjoyable as watching Katie laugh is seeing the chain reaction that follows. Once she gets started, it's only a matter of time before we're all hopelessly caught up in the fun. Even her younger sister, who sometimes looks on disapprovingly as Katie lapses into one of her laughing fits, eventually caves in and joins the party.

Almost anything can tickle her funny bone, but TV commercials seem to work best. She really likes the one where the doting parents try to capture their baby's first words with the video camera. At the big moment, the baby looks straight into the lens and says, in quite the proper adult voice, "Oh, Daddy, you paid too much for that camcorder." That little piece of cinemagic is enough to send Katie into wacky-spasms. Also, anything on America's Funniest Home Videos will do the trick, and people tripping or falling are reliable standbys.

If laughter is the best medicine, our home is a twenty-four-hour pharmacy.

The Kids Pull a Fast One

There has been wailing and gnashing of teeth lately at our house. My wife is wailing and I'm gnashing. Our children—on their own and without so much as a how-do-you-do—have decided to get older. The very nerve.

Katie and Amy have started high school and middle school. This was not supposed to happen. I thought my children would always be cuddly little people who asked me to buy them Happy Meals. Instead, my older daughter came home and told me about the drug-sniffing dog that visited her school, and my younger child is getting phone calls from (deep breath ... go to my happy place) a boy.

"Now just a minute," I implore in my wife's general direction. "Didn't you just birth these children? Wasn't I whining about the price of diapers only last week? Aren't we still making payments on the pediatrician's Lexus?

"And, by the way, I don't remember giving them permission to shave their legs."

That's because they didn't ask for my permission, she said. Seems it was one of those mother-daughter executive decisions. Apparently I've been out of the loop for a while now. It's been one reeling executive decision after another. (I wasn't even consulted when the green fingernail polish was approved.) Now look what's happened—they're hobnobbing with middle-schoolers and high-schoolers.

My wife, of all people, should have seen this coming, but she was caught off guard even more than I. She came to me the other night and placed her face directly between me and the television. She stared at me with misty eyes.

I smiled, thinking, how sweet—we are having a special moment.

"I'm losing my babies," she said.

Oops. Bad read.

"You're not losing your babies," I said. "Think about it. They're only a day older than they were yesterday. You weren't losing them yesterday, were you?"

Again, the misty eyes.

"You could never be a mother," she said, and she walked away to stare at her sleeping children.

For their part, the girls were handling the upheaval pretty well. Katie was experiencing a pinch of freshman anxiety. Some of her fears were the same ones she expressed when she graduated from kindergarten to first grade—not being able to find the right class-room, or not knowing some subject matter the teacher might expect her to have learned already. If Amy had any misgivings about going to middle school, I never heard them. She was sleeping soundly when I went in to check on her the night before the first day of school.

The next afternoon, I asked Katie how her day had gone. "Fine," she said. Bored. Nonchalant.

"Just fine?"

"Fine."

Amy, on the other hand, told me all about her new teachers, in-cluding the gym instructor who barked out commands like a drill sergeant, and about some new friends she'd made.

I expected my wife's worrisome mood to have lifted, seeing that her children had survived the first day of school in good emotional shape. No such luck. She had moved on to some new burden. She is a mother.

What, Me Worry?

There are some people who are not beset with anxiety. Amy, our eleven-year-old, is such a carefree creature. This is a source of some annoyance for my wife, whose job it is to make sure each of us is sufficiently worried about something.

"Our daughter has a spelling test tomorrow," she says to me as I peer into the refrigerator.

"Really?" My gaze locks on the Breyers vanilla ice cream. Molecules of happiness explode inside me.

"Well? Aren't you worried?"

"About what?"

"About your daughter's spelling test."

"Should I be worried?"

"Well, somebody around here needs to worry about these things."

"I've got great news, honey," I say, scooping out a yummy blend of pure sugar, saturated fat and genuine vanilla-bean specks. "The girls and I took a vote, and we elected you Designated Worrier."

Silence. The Breyers isn't the only chilly thing in the room.

Luckily for me, Amy cartwheels into the kitchen, temporarily distracting her mom. "Are you ready for your spelling test?" she asks the slender bouncing person, who says, "Watch me do a quadruple-flying-half-twist-from-the-tuck-somersault."

"Watch me pull my hair out," says her mom, turning the skunk eye back on me.

Amy completes her tumbling routine with a curtsy and bounds back toward her room. We're hopeful she will emerge with a spelling book but aren't holding our breath. She is easily distracted, and any number of interesting side roads lie on the stretch between the kitchen and her bedroom. Her mother will follow in a couple of minutes and find Amy feeding her hermit crabs, listening to her radio or throwing rolled-up socks across the hall into her sister's room—anything but spelling.

"Amy, your spelling."

"Oh, yeah!" she says, genuinely surprised at her forgetfulness.

Amy doesn't worry about tests, projects or deadlines. She believes these things will take care of themselves. She's one of the few people I know who takes to heart the simple advice, "Don't worry." She cares about things, but she doesn't sweat the details. If she worries about anything, it's other people's feelings. Her mission is to make everybody in the room feel loved. She especially showers affection on young children and old people. Perhaps that's because she identifies with them—children who haven't yet learned to worry, and old people who have learned that time is too valuable to waste being anxious.

Debbie calls out Amy's study words, and Amy dutifully spells them again and again until her mom is satisfied. Of course, this will not keep her from worrying about Amy's spelling test, not until the grade comes back. And it is almost always a good grade. "See, honey," I'm inclined to say on those occasions, "all that worry for nothing!"

"Wrong," she says. "All that worry for an 'A.'"

Yes, all that worry for an "A," as in Amy.

March Madness

Spring is in the air, and a not-so-young man's fancy turns to thoughts of critters. It's the time of year when my yard becomes an all-you-can-eat salad bar for the bunnies living in the woods bordering our backyard. When I turn into the driveway at night and the headlights sweep across the yard, I see rabbits loitering about my property like teenagers in a mall parking lot, disrespecting the quality of my dandelions. It is at this moment that our trusty golden retriever, Millie, explodes out of the garage, sending rabbits scampering in every direction. Paralyzed by the chaos, Millie trembles and points toward the woods. "R-r-rabbits," she seems to be saying.

Rabbits aren't the only rodents that inhabit my yard. So do moles. My backyard is a mole retirement community. Their holes can disable a riding lawn mower. Moles have a subway system that would make New Yorkers envious. I imagine little moles chomping on cigars, their trousers pulled up around their armpits, riding around in subterranean passageways in a little mole golf cart with the left turn signal constantly blinking. On the back of the cart is a bumper sticker: "Let Me Tell You About My Grandmoles."

Millie caught a mole once and carried it back to her bed and slept beside it all night. Sadly, this behavior has become creepily habitual. She kills small mammals, then feels guilty and tries to make up for it by offering them a warm bed and a couple of dog-chow nuggets.

Rabbits and moles are a nuisance, but they don't keep me awake at night. Snakes, on the other hand, get into my mind and stay there.

A snake-event happened to us about this time a few years ago. We were watching the NCAA basketball championship on TV. My wife was on the couch, and I was stretched out on the floor. Amy, who was supposed to be in bed, appeared in the doorway and asked to stay up for a while. I was focused on the game, so I only halfway heard the conversation between my daughter and her mother. I did, of course, hear her mother scream.

"AMYTHERE'SASNAKEONTHEFLOORJUMPUPHERE-NOWBEFOREITBITESYOUITHINKI'MHYPERVENTILAT-ING!!!"

Talk about your March Madness.

In that first moment I didn't know why she was screaming—the game was not that exciting—but when I saw my wife and daughter standing on the back of the couch, clinging to each other and shrieking, I figured it out: It must be the snake slithering out from under the couch.

My first thought was this: There's a snake on my floor. My second thought was this: I am on the floor. My third thought was this: Get off the floor. (My wife, to her credit, managed to bypass thoughts one and two and proceed directly to "get on the ceiling.")

The startled little black snake turned toward the hallway. I jumped up, shut the door and cornered the snake, which was not happy. It coiled. It hissed. It was not as agitated, however, as my wife, who managed to ascend to theretofore untapped decibel levels.

"AIIIEEE!" she said.

"Honey, get me a pillow case!" I yelled.

"AIIIEEE!" my wife said. (Translation: "The pillow cases are in the hall closet. The snake is between me and the hall closet. Do I need to draw you a picture?")

"Honey, get me a trash bag!" I begged.

"AIIIEEE!" said my wife. (Translation: "I'm fine here on the back of the couch.")

"Honey, if we don't catch this snake right now, he's going to disappear somewhere in this house, and then we'll have to move!"

"AIIIEEE!" my wife and daughter said in unison. (Translation: "Why did YOU let this happen?")

She got the trash bag for me. How she managed to levitate herself from the couch to the kitchen cabinet, I'll never know. The woman was motivated.

We bagged the little snake and released him at the edge of the woods. Millie stood at some distance behind me and barked threateningly. The rabbits giggled.

Later that night, I said to my wife, "When you see one snake, that means there are probably more around."

"We're moving," she said. (Translation: "AIIIEEE!")

Her Hypertension's Killing Me

My wife has been diagnosed with high blood pressure, which stresses me out. In theory, it is her tension, not mine, with which we should be concerned, but she's not worried. "It's just a little pill I have to take in the morning," she says. This from a woman who loses sleep when the mini-blinds are out of parallel.

"Honey," I protest, "this is hypertension we're talking about—from 'hyper,' meaning 'excessive,' and 'tension,' meaning 'the condition of being stretched.' Your doctor is saying you are excessively stretched out. This doesn't sound good for my mental health."

"Okay," she says. "We'll return this diagnosis and see if the doctor can offer us a good deal on something else—say, a bleeding ulcer."

Ironically, my wife, who is tranquilly challenged, is handling the high blood pressure thing with uncharacteristic calm. She's the first to tell you it's the little things—like a slow Sunday driver—that get her stress meter up and spinning. During a major crisis, however, she is a rock, calming hysterical people and barking commands like a NASA flight director. When the threat of a tornado forced a group of mothers, gymnastics instructors and weeping little girls to cower in two small restrooms, she was cool-headed. When she thought we might get home too late to watch the Friends wedding on TV, she got a little freaked out.

She checks her blood pressure almost nightly, then calls her parents to discuss the ups and downs of systolics and diastolics. The other night, I walked into the den, and she was lying motionless on the couch, staring at the ceiling, doing absolutely nothing—no TV, no magazine, no nothing.

"What?" I asked.

"I'm powering down before I take my blood pressure reading," she said.

I pointed out the flaw in her system. "Just so I understand—you run around all day doing stressful stuff, then you force yourself into a state of relaxation just before you slap the cuff on, and that's your official reading for the day?"

"Works for me," she said.

So she's dealing with this thing quite nicely, while my blood pressure is inching up from worrying about hers. I think it's because her hypertension makes me feel old. High blood pressure was something only "old people" had when I was a kid. When I went to my grandparents' house and saw the little cityscape of medicine bottles on their kitchen table, it felt a little spooky. Now those medicine bottles are starting to show up on my table, and some are for me. Getting old worries me. My heart speeds up when I think about my children growing up and leaving home or when the optometrist tells me I need bifocals.

So when I, in a thoughtful and loving manner, begin to lecture my wife about having a short fuse when she gets behind a slow driver, she's likely to turn to me and say, because she's just that way, "Honey, is that an age spot on the back of your hand?"

Doggone Van

As I stand by the mailbox, looking at the payment book for my wife's new previously owned minivan, basking in the afterglow of my generous nature, I am struck by a suddenly urgent question: How am I going to transport my dog to the vet?

It didn't occur to me when buying the newer van that we no longer had a vehicle we were willing to put the dog in. I've never been in this position before. We've always had at least one vehicle that was dog-worthy.

Here's the problem: We have two vehicles—one is my wife's new minivan, and the other is her old Honda Accord, which I inherited. My dog is a seventy-five-pound, windshield-licking, upholstery-slobbering sweetheart of a golden retriever. She won't fit in the Honda, and I don't even joke with my wife about letting the dog ride in her new van.

Millie only rides in a vehicle if she's sick or going fishing. She has learned to distinguish between the two. Despite the fact that she is a golden retriever but can't grasp the concept of retrieving, she is smart enough to know that if she gets into a vehicle and I'm not holding a fishing rod, the next thing she'll see will be a large man wanting to take her temperature with something, ironically enough, resembling a fishing rod.

So what to do? I've thought about getting her a motorcycle sidecar. I can visualize it: speeding along the four-lane, my dog's sidecar attached to the minivan, my children hanging out the window shouting encouragement to the dog, Millie decked out in goggles and a red flowing scarf, her fur dancing in the wind. I also can visualize a lawsuit when Millie leans out to lick a pedestrian at fifty-five miles per hour.

Maybe I should just get an old pickup truck. I've been threatening to do this for the last fifteen years. "Every man needs a truck," I say to no one in particular, although my spouse is the only person in the room.

"Why?" she asks.

"To haul stuff."

"What kind of stuff?"

"You know ... stuff."

"Stuff?"

I give up. If you have to explain it, it spoils the whole thing.

There are two females at our house, however, who are solidly behind my truck-ownership aspirations. One is Millie, who gets jealous when she sees a certain fellow drive past our house with a pickup full of happy barking dogs. She gazes wistfully after them. It must be like going on a hayride every day.

The other female at our house who would dearly love to see me in a pickup is our daughter Katie, who is about to turn fifteen. If I get a truck, then the Honda will pass to her, or so she believes. She doesn't understand that she's not ready to drive. I, on the other hand, know this because I watched her race go-carts at the beach recently. Katie puts the speed in speedway. She makes the Indy 500 look like a Roman chariot race now. She makes Jeff Gordon look like the Rainbow Tortoise.

Still, it would be good to be the owner of a rickety old pickup ... you know, to haul stuff. As I stand beside the mailbox pondering these things, I remember the fat little payment book in my hand. Financial reality lands with a thud.

Millie sidles up and licks my hand. I scratch her ears. "How do you feel about a U-Haul, girl?"

Shooting Baskets, Taking Stock

I'll miss some things about living at 1001 Green Willow Trail:

... sorting through my thoughts while shooting free throws in the driveway.

... admiring our deck and every one of the thousand nails my wife and I hammered into it. I'll also miss the treehouse I built for my kids (which was really a gift to myself).

... sitting on the back porch and watching thunderstorms roll in.

... building a fire on a rainy Saturday afternoon and watching a good college football game on TV.

... chasing my laughing children down the hallway.

... waking my wife from her slumber on the sofa to tell her that Sid Bream was safe at the plate and the Braves won the National League Pennant.

... standing in the road and admiring my half-acre after a grimy but satisfying day of yard work.

... taking walks around the subdivision with my wife.

... showing people the exact spot where a snake slithered out from under our couch one March night and my wife and daughter ascended instantly to the back of the couch.

... riding my bike to Rice Cemetery and visiting the residents.

... tromping through the woods with my kids and their cousins and swinging them from an old rope over the creek.

... parking in my garage and walking into my house without getting wet.

... driving to the crossroads store on a Saturday morning to buy gas for the lawn mower.

... teasing our neighbor when she mows her lawn and waving her over to cut ours.

... living across the street from a guy who knows everything there is to know about fixing a lawn mower.

... the little utility building my friend Eddie and I assembled one sweltering afternoon.

... the quiet that settles like a blanket over our subdivision when the sun goes down.

When we move in a couple of weeks, we'll be leaving behind a house that has been our home for more than ten years. Our oldest was about to enter kindergarten when we moved here. She's driving now. Our youngest was a toddler. There was no gray on my head, and my wife didn't ask for the reading glasses with her morning paper.

We'll soon load up the furniture, clothes, photo albums, the washer and dryer, and we'll move to another place. I'll say goodbye to Green Willow Trail, but I won't say goodbye to the best parts about living there. Those go with me, and their names are Debbie, Katie and Amy.

Morning People

I am not a morning person, but on occasion I am out there with the early risers. Today I was chauffeuring my wife to work because her car was in the shop. After dropping her off, I drove up the interstate, impersonating a morning person, and witnessed a sunrise—radiant pinks and blues that reveal themselves only at dawn, part of an awakening world that reveals itself while I sleep.

I should get up early and take in the glory of daybreak more often, but I'm not wired for it. As a teenager, I stole every extra minute of sleep I could, driving my dad crazy. He was a lifelong early riser, the result—literally—of getting up with the chickens to pick cotton and, for the rest of his working life, punching a time clock at the Fiberglas plant. He warned me that sleeping late would lead to no good and predicted I would eventually become a morning person like him. I still want to sleep late and stay up late.

My wife is a morning person. She gets up early in order to move unhurried through her routine. At 5:15 AM, the television in our bedroom clicks on, and the first voices I hear in the flickering gloom are those of Gordon, Stacy and Dale, who redundantly offer up headlines, weather and traffic with a cheeriness that borders on inconsiderate. My wife spends the first twenty minutes of her day in the company of these on-air optimists and has grown attached to them. Lately she frets that Gordon is only pretending (and not very well) to like Stacy. Debbie remarks on this as a smiling Dale promises to give us the bus-stop forecast "right after this."

When she turns off the TV and heads for the shower, I have twenty minutes of bonus sleep before the women in my house commence a morning ritual that involves blow-dryers, a squeaky ironing board, drawers being opened then slammed, shoes clomping on wood floors, animated discussions about what looks good with what, perfume being spritzed in the air and walked through, and vigorous tooth-brushing and spitting.

I can sleep through most of it. My brain is adept at filtering out morning noise. If a daughter yells from down the hall, "Where's my pink top?" I will not skip a snore even as my wife, who is rummaging like a starved raccoon through a jewelry box filled with shiny clinking metal things, yells back:

"Which pink top?"

"The one I like."

"The one you really like?"

"No, the one I kind of like, but not a whole lot, but more than the one I like just a little."

"Oh, that one—it's under the white towel in the blue laundry basket behind the door beside the red laundry basket where you'll also find a pair of socks you will need for cheerleading tomorrow."

"Thanks, Mom! How do you always know?"

"It's my job."

Music to my ears. As long as someone else worries about these things, I can sleep soundly. However, I would appreciate a wakeup call in twenty minutes. I want to see if Gordon is getting too thin on his new diet. I worry.

The Year of Last Things

It is the Year of Last Things at our house. Amy, the baby, is a senior in high school. Over the next few months, she will be doing some things for the very last time. The import of each last thing will be mournfully noted by her mother.

This gloomy observance began a few months ago when Debbie and Lisa, our neighbor, whose son is also a senior and the youngest in his family, came together in the yard to talk about the impending season of maternal misery.

"I'm going to be an emotional basket case the whole year," Lisa said.

"You'd better not even look at me the wrong way," said Debbie, "or I'll start boohooing."

Lisa's husband, John, and I exchanged knowing glances. We had seen it before. We knew better than to tease too much. From personal experience, and from John's forays into the woods as an experienced outdoorsman, we understood that you don't get between a mother and her cub.

Amy cheered at her final high school football game Friday night. She has been a cheerleader for most of her life. In fact, when she was born, she bounced into the delivery room with a flourish and a backflip and a perky admonition that "all for Amy stand up and holler!" My wife mumbled something about having hollered enough for one day. Over the years, every time Amy or Katie appeared in public (for spelling bees, cheerleading competitions, piano concerts, dance recitals, having their nails done) their mother was front and center, their loyal and loudest fan.

For more than twenty years, she has made it her mission to know the names of our children's friends, to memorize their schedules, prod them in their schoolwork and activities, and listen when they needed to talk. She has done all the hard work and never resented it when I stepped in at moments of celebration to steal the first hugs from my girls. But when they needed a sympathetic shoulder because they were disappointed, afraid or brokenhearted, it was their mother who was first in line, arms open wide. She has invested herself completely in their well-being. She is a good mother.

This is our second journey through the Year of Last Things. We are understanding again that graduation from high school is an important threshold. Things change significantly when they go off to college, even if it's only twenty minutes away. Our involvement in their daily lives suddenly drops off. Katie lives away from home these days. Her friends are people we didn't watch grow up. She inhabits a world apart from ours, one in which she makes most of the big decisions, and one from which she doesn't come home each night.

That's why this is a bittersweet time for Amy's mom, this Year of Last Things. The adventure that awaits our daughter is precisely what we always wanted for her. But things will never be the same.

Still, there's this: Every morning when I walk out of the house, I look forward to returning home at the end of the day. And so it is for our children: The best part of leaving home is coming back, and that's because Mom is there. She's always there.

Have a Coke and a Smile

Ask most any man, and he'll likely tell you he does some of his best thinking while operating the lawn mower. It doesn't matter if we're pushing or riding—we're not all that picky when it comes to thinking. There's something meditative about cutting a path through the tall grass—see the row, mow the row, turn ... see the row, mow the row, turn.

And on and on it goes, week after week, year after year, until we wake up and behold that regal rolling lawn in the sky. It's a beautiful thing. Piloting our lawn mowers, with no television to distract us, we're left with nothing to do but carve perfect geometric patterns in our yards and—if we're not chewing gum—to think.

This is what I thought about recently while mowing my lawn: I don't consciously try to embarrass my family. It just happens.

A few weeks ago, my wife and I took a stroll around the block. On the home stretch, we stopped at the drug store to pick up a household item or two. Once inside, I discovered that the entire Coke family of products was on sale, so I decided I needed no less than four fridge-packs, which comes to exactly forty-eight cans of soft drink.

Four soft-drink fridgepacks are not unmanageable if you're pushing them in a shopping cart, but they are like a herd of lunging elephant seals if you try to walk home with them over a distance of two blocks.

Which is exactly what we did. My wife, ever thoughtful to remind me that I do my best thinking on a lawn mower but that I was not on a lawn mower and therefore should not attempt to do any thinking, asked me what I was thinking.

"I'm thinking about you, honey," I said, immediately pleased with myself.

"That's not what I meant," she replied, not even bothering to roll her eyes. "How are you going to get all these cans home? We're walking, remember?"

"Of course I remember," I said. My manhood was deeply wounded. "Don't worry, woman. I'm strong."

So down the sidewalk we trudged. She was toting three plastic bags filled with prescription drugs and assorted household necessaries, and I schlepped my four fridgepacks of Coca-Cola products. I looked like a beast of burden ascending a volcano in a Tarzan movie.

We passed our neighbor's house. As fate would have it, they were having a soirée, and folks were enjoying themselves on the front porch. I thought it neighborly of them to wave at exactly the moment I paused in order to redistribute the weight of my Coke products (as I could no longer feel the ends of my fingers).

I thought to exchange a few pleasantries with the revelers, but when I looked up, I saw that my wife had abandoned me and was closing fast on our front walk. I couldn't exactly wave to the party people, but I did manage a quick dip and nod, and then I hurried to catch up before my wife could lock me out of the house.

I still don't understand what the big deal was. I mean—and I'm speaking hypothetically here—would she be embarrassed if she saw me riding my lawn mower down the sidewalk while simultaneously towing a push mower, trundling the two blocks to the hardware store, in broad daylight in front of everybody, wearing NASCAR-grade ear protection? Would that be embarrassing?

In my defense, when that seemed like a perfectly reasonable idea to me, I wasn't mowing the lawn.

A Walk Around the Block

It was a sunny Sunday afternoon, and I talked my wife into taking a walk around the block with me. She enjoys a nice walk, but not if it's too cold (or too warm, or too windy, or too early or late, or if she's busy doing something more important). Otherwise, she's always up for a walk (unless her supper hasn't had time to settle).

For me, the walk is about the journey—ambling, taking in the scenery, observing nature's critters in their wooded habitats, throwing a foam football at a manhole cover and celebrating like I've won a million dollars when I hit one. For me, to walk is to meander from one side of the street to the other in a never-ending quest to see what's on the other side. If you ask me why the chicken crossed the road, I'll probably stop in my tracks and give the question some serious thought.

For my wife, however, the walk is not about the journey; it is about getting from point A to point B, even if point B is the same place from which she started. For her, a walk should have a logical, profitable purpose, such as exploring a house that is under construction—that, or physical fitness. When she walks with her health in mind, she strikes a vigorous pace that challenges my aging knees. She really gets it going, with her arms and legs pumping like Fred Flintstone in his rock-mobile when he's late for bowling night with Barney. Steely concentration takes hold, and woe be unto any creature that gets between her and point B. The woman moves fast and in a straight line.

I have noticed recently, however, a hairline crack in her military discipline. Dried acorns dot the road and sidewalk along our route, and she delights in stomping them and hearing them explode like firecrackers. In these unguarded moments of merriment, she has been known to temporarily lose sight of point B.

Sometimes, when we've almost completed our circuit around the neighborhood, she slows down, no longer in a big hurry. This is the part of our walk I most enjoy, the part where she starts talking about her day, our children, the neighbors' pretty flowers, or about nothing in particular. We just talk, and the walk becomes a comfortable vehicle for our conversation. The pace relaxes, and a spinning world slows down.

I am about the journey, and she is about the destination. Without my stops along the way, her destination might be an efficient but boring place. And without her sense of destination, my journey would be aimless.

Walking with her reminds me of these things.

The Gift

Saturday was a gift. In my book, all Saturdays are gifts, but some have more of the good stuff than others. Last Saturday was filled to the brim with the good stuff.

In a winter that has been by turns either clear and frigid or wet and mild, Saturday dawned bright, with the promise of afternoon temperatures in the mid-sixties. The night before, I had announced my intention to strip the house of Christmas decorations, but as the air warmed I wanted to be outside on a day that felt more like early October than late December.

And so outside I went. I spent the afternoon running the lawn mower over the quilt of oak leaves on my front lawn. The Snapper chewed them up and spat them out in jagged flakes; the leaves were but remnants of themselves. Two or three passes over the same spot, and the whirling blade, like some cyclonic contraption in a robot competition, sliced and diced the dry leaves to a consistency as fine as sprinkled cinnamon. The dusty brown nutrient settled on optimistic green shoots of grass. (This is about as close as I come to waxing poetic on the joy of landscaping.)

Earlier that morning I helped take down the Christmas trees, much to my wife's pleasure. In exchange, she agreed to take the wheel of the Snapper while I raked the areas of the yard the mower couldn't reach. With both of us working, we made a decent dent in the season's accumulation. Even though the sun never got high in the midwinter sky—I constantly was shielding my eyes—its warmth on my back made even the repetitive task of raking leaves a pleasurable chore. I simply did not want the day to end. If the sun had stayed aloft, as it does in northern latitudes this time of the year, I believe I could have stayed in my yard until New Year's Day.

Saturday reminded me of why I am glad to be alive. Nothing spectacular happened. We didn't win the Publishers Clearing House Sweepstakes, and I didn't stumble upon the fountain of youth. But I did rediscover the joy of working in my own yard, of seeing my family safe and sound, of knowing that, at least for a warm Saturday in December, all was well.

Three years ago, I had colon cancer. After successful surgery to remove the tumor, I took six months of precautionary chemotherapy. There were moments during those six months when I felt sorry for myself, but there were many more moments when I understood how fortunate I was—not for surviving cancer, because that could come again, because something eventually will come—but for being loved, for being in this family, for being in this place and time.

During those six months, I set about building a low wall along the curved edge of my driveway. Building that wall—not keeping the monthly appointments with the chemicals—was my real therapy. I looked forward to the days when I felt strong enough to be out in my yard, taking pickax to tree roots and unearthing long-buried concrete blocks.

I promised myself that I would never again resent yard work, that I would not take for granted the gift of working hard, of breathing leaf dust, of sweating in the sun. Every time I see my chemo wall,

I remember the promise.

Much of life is uncertain, but I am certain of this moment. It is a gift.

Living Large with Teddy Wayne Mitchell

We were driving near downtown Greenville and passed a cemetery I often walk through while on my lunch hour. I'll sometimes sit on a bench beneath an oak tree there and think. I pointed to the cemetery and began telling my family what a peaceful place it is for me, a mental oasis. My children's eyes glazed over. They murmured something indistinct, a hazy acknowledgment of their father's tendency to prattle on … blah, blah … snooze.

The impulse to ramble on is strong. I am sometimes like Clark Griswold, trudging through waist-deep snow, leading his family on a quest for The Perfect Family Christmas Tree, holding forth on the virtues of kith and kin even as his daughter's eyeballs freeze over.

My children didn't always think me boring. When they were young and I still tucked them in at night, they begged for a bedtime story, preferably "something about when you were a little kid." They especially enjoyed tales of my boyhood friend and world-class daredevil, Teddy Wayne Mitchell.

The stories about Teddy Wayne Mitchell (always the full name, just like "Billy Ray Cyrus") were packed with adventure. There was the time Teddy Wayne Mitchell, a few years older, dared me, a six-year-old, to punch my fist through a glass door; I did, and the gush of blood was impressive. Another time, while demonstrating the holy ordinance of baptism, he nearly drowned me in the bathtub, causing my mother to raise a high holy ruckus and chase him home.

There was also the time my mom was busy hosting a Stanley party, and Teddy Wayne Mitchell pushed me, in a homemade go-cart with no brakes, down a hill into oncoming traffic. I survived unscathed. Then there was the morning we were exploring in the woods and he plucked me up and held me over an abandoned well and told me he was going to drop me down the hole and leave my carcass for the possums. He didn't. One summer evening, he filled a peach basket with toads and dumped them on my mom's living room floor. Never again do I expect I'll see a hundred warty reptiles in a living room, all of them advancing on my screaming mother.

Even when Teddy Wayne Mitchell's escapades threatened my personal safety or led me down paths of sin, he was still my best friend. Every time my life flashed before my eyes, he was at my side, laughing, clapping me on the back and running off toward the next adventure with me blissfully in pursuit. Despite his penchant for terrorizing me, I adored him. He could have chosen to spend his time with anybody; instead, he ran from across the road and knocked on our door and asked my mom if I could come out and play. Even at six, I understood loyalty.

I don't remember when I stopped telling my kids Teddy Wayne Mitchell stories. Nowadays, every once in a while, I fade to blue when I contemplate my diminishing relevance in my daughters' lives. As my little girls have become young women, my role as father has evolved. No longer do I get down in the floor with them to serve as a base for their daring acrobatics. Instead, I try to be an emotional base, a shoulder to cry on, a safe place to come home.

When my wife senses I'm feeling disconnected from my children, she reminds me that the girls still talk fondly about tromping through the woods with their dad and swinging across the creek on a rope. It doesn't rise to the level of Teddy Wayne Mitchell lore, but perhaps the memory will make for a bedtime story to help children yet to be born fall asleep with happy hearts.

Mom's Big Ol' Pot of Chili

As I write this while sitting on my living room couch, aroma molecules from a bubbling pot of chili-and-beans float in the air, traveling to me from the kitchen along the furnace-warmed currents of our home. They waft, tantalizing, about my nose. Outside, it is twenty-seven degrees. From my vantage point by the window, a brittle blanket of ice covers the earth as far as I can see.

The weatherman warns that more frozen stuff is on the way. I worry that my old oaks won't take the extra weight. I feel guilty because I can stay at home when others must work. Still, wishing for snow is a childhood indulgence I have never relinquished. If growing up means never again to hope for snow, then I will happily revert to twelve years old.

With the ice on the trees and a steaming pot of chili on the stove, it would be hard to draw a cozier scene. The hearty goodness simmering in the kitchen isn't your average pot of chili—it is, in fact, a Big Ol' Pot of Chili. My wife, the creator of the Big Ol' Pot of Chili, was the one who coined the description, which now enjoys common usage at our house. We can't resist the urge to tease her with her own words. When she suggests cooking a pot of chili, my daughters and I make conspiratorial eye contact and reply: "Not just any pot of chili—no, a Big Ol' Pot of Chili!" We delight in our wit. My wife rolls her eyes. (She has a lot of practice.) She leaves us to our amusement and goes off to prepare her signature masterpiece.

Watching her pull it all together is free entertainment. She methodically places the ingredients around her—ground beef, tomatoes, kidney beans, onions, bell peppers, spices (a dab, a dash, no measuring spoons; this recipe is accomplished by feel) and launches her attack. Like a game show contestant racing the clock, her tempo is breakneck. In a blur of hands and utensils, meat gets browned, cans get opened and dumped, and produce gets chopped and diced. Her eyes grow large with focus, and the tendons in her jaw strain as she abuses the hand-operated dicer, her arms pounding like pistons, punishing a poor onion into submission. All the ingredients go into … yes, a big ol' pot, where they stew away all afternoon, stirred occasionally with a big ol' spoon. Afterwards, the pleasing aroma of onions and chili peppers slow-cooking on the stove gives one pause to consider an existential question: Does it get any better than this?

Mom's Big Ol' Pot of Chili has achieved iconic status. Like a turkey in the oven on Thanksgiving, the cooking of chili endows the day with a special quality. A chili day might occur when there's a big football game on television, or, like today, when a winter storm slows the world to a snow-crunching halt. In the last couple of years, another occasion has achieved status worthy of a chili day, and that's when Katie fetches home a ravenous band of college friends whose taste buds have been dulled by cafeteria fare.

Katie was downcast when the ice storm prevented her from driving home and partaking of the event that is her mom's chili. Mom was sad, too; no matter how satisfying the supper, she's never quite full when someone is absent from the circle. A mother's love, the secret ingredient in her Big Ol' Pot of Chili, seasons our lives and keeps the circle unbroken.

No Peas Please

It's puzzling what the mind chooses to remember. For instance, I know, from eavesdropping on a conversation, that a friend's infant daughter has begun eating baby food. Every Monday, her parents introduce her to a new variety of strained vegetable. She recently sampled green peas and was unimpressed. Her sympathetic father observed that if one mixes a green pea with any other food, then the whole meal is besmirched with the aftertaste of green peas. He believes that little green spheroid is a potent thing, and even a pound of mashed potatoes and gravy can't overcome the twang of a single

English pea.

Let's set aside the argument of whether he's right. Let's disregard the fact that my wife, to whom he was saying this, agrees that a green pea is the canker of the vegetable world. Let's not even talk about the fact that when she is on the phone placing a takeout order for vegetable fried rice, an Abbot and Costello routine ensues:

"I'd like that without green peas, please."

"Green peas, please?"

"No. No green peas, please."

"No green peas?"

"Yes. No green peas."

"No?"

"No green peas. Yes."

"Yes?"

"No."

I am in no position to judge. I admit to pulling up to the drive-through at McDonald's and ordering the two-cheeseburger meal, minus the cheese.

I also cannot speak of peas without recalling the time in fifth grade when I had to write, 500 times, "I will not shoot peas under the table."

But I digress. The point is this: I will always remember, long after my friend's child is grown, that every Monday her parents tried out a new kind of mushed-up vegetable on her (met with a spectacular yucky face, no doubt, as I recall from feeding strained green beans to my children).

Why would my mind decide to remember that particular snippet? Why was the conversation noteworthy enough to settle down in an overstuffed chair in a corner of my brain? How was it I could remember nothing of what the ambassador from Belgium said that morning on "Meet the Press," but I could not forget that if you have a single pea floating like a frog's eye in your vegetable soup, then it might as well be a hundred-percent pea soup?

My brain just works that way. I am at the mercy of the sweet old librarian who lives in my head, the one who sifts through the trainload of stuff that passes through each day, deciding whether to file or toss.

I remember some mundane things, and I forget some pretty important events. I remember staring dumbstruck at my younger brother Rusty's umbilical cord when my mom brought him home from the hospital, but I don't remember noticing him again until he was old enough to play baseball with me.

I also remember a time from my childhood when my cousin Gary spent the night with me, and, after we had grown quiet, and each thought the other asleep, we heard, drifting in from the television in the living room, a Green Giant canned corn commercial, followed by the catchy jingle, "In the valley of the jolly ... ," at which point we both sang softly, "Ho, ho, ho." We started giggling, and it was a long time before we fell asleep.

Two peas in a pod, we were.

Remains of a Rainy Day

It dawned rainy. My kind of day.

I enjoy the sun as much as anyone. Many are the times I've lingered late in the yard after a day of mowing and raking, soaking up the waning moments of a warm afternoon.

But I enjoy the rain, too. A rainy day is possessed of an insulating quality. It shushes the world. It hints of the wellspring of our existence, speaking in a language that even unborn children understand. Water, the font of our biology, sings to us of its sustenance—through the pounding of ocean surf, the gurgling of woodland creek, the patter of rain on a rusting tin roof.

There are few experiences more calming than to wake to the quietness of rain falling from above. Greeting such mornings when I was a boy, I would outfit myself in poncho and rubber boots and strike out to the woods. A rainy day meant I would be the lone human in the woods. On a rainy day, the woods were a still place, a muffled cocoon.

It was that kind of day. I drove to town on errands, taking my time, synchronizing my internal clock to the slap of windshield wipers. At each stop, I turned off the motor and lingered in the car— not to avoid getting wet, but because I wanted to hear the sound of rain on the roof.

Later, I suggested to my wife that it would be a good day to drive up into the mountains. I didn't expect we'd see much, but I convinced her there aren't many things more peaceful than taking a leisurely drive in an easy rain.

It was late afternoon when we finally were on our way, and the rain played out before we left the foothills behind and began our ascent up the Greenville County side of the Appalachian Range. Under gray skies and patchy fog, we made our way up a winding slope. We had no hint of the spectacle that awaited us.

By the time we neared the summit of Caesar's Head, most of the day was spent. In those final hairpin turns before we reached the top, we could see, through the trees, a mist beginning to enshroud the mountain. We parked near the three or four vehicles remaining at the visitor's center and walked quickly to the viewing area, a section of rock that is the crown of Caesar's Head, a vista that normally affords a stomach-stealing panorama onto granite-faced peaks, rolling hills and fertile valleys.

What we saw from the precipice stunned us. We found ourselves gazing across the vast expanse of a mountain-lined bowl, tens of miles across, and the bowl was filled nearly to the brim with milk. It wasn't milk, of course, but the perfectly flat top of an opalescent cloud. Distant peaks rose like mossy icebergs from the windswept sea of white. The whiteness could swallow us, I thought. It appeared infinitely deep, but I heard the faint roar of water, a river flowing somewhere in the depth.

There were just a few people there to experience it with us. An older man told us he had stood at the spot a hundred times and never seen anything like it. A woman whispered, "Have we died and gone to heaven?"

I've never been able to understand the appeal of strolling on streets of gold, but this was something I could wrap my imagination around—this, the remains of a rainy day.

Home: Do Not Disturb

I am sitting in a hotel room a couple of hundred miles from home, and I don't like it.

The older I get, the more anxious I am about overnight work trips. If a trip is looming, I'll slip into a funk the week before. On my last day at the office, I clean off my desk in the event I don't make it back; I don't want to be a burden to my coworkers. Sometimes I'll feel ill the day before I'm supposed to leave, as if a cold might be coming on. Sometimes I secretly hope I will get a little sick, but not too sick. Then I chastise myself for thinking such a thing, because you should be careful what you wish for.

As I write this, I'm sitting at a functional desk in a perfectly adequate room with two double beds covered with green and yellow bedspreads. On the other side of the wall, there's another room with identical furniture and green and yellow bedspreads, only in reverse. I am snacking on a bag of Fritos and Diet Coke, which I bought at a convenience store in the hope that familiar food would make this room feel more like home. It does not.

I am misplaced.

My aversion to being away from home has gotten worse in recent years. I'm a creature of habit, and sliding a magnetic card into a door and waiting for a green light to glow is not one of my habits. When I'm home, I follow the same routine every night. I feed my two dogs, Millie and Gabbie, and give them doggie treats in an attempt to make up for the times I don't walk them. I feed the cat, which my wife calls Puddin' but I simply refer to as The Cat. Then I lock the doors, turn down the thermostats, go to bed and wait for everyone else to fall asleep. I need to be the last one to go to sleep.

Being on the road messes with all that.

When I'm away, my wife feeds the animals, and when I call home, I may ask if the dogs have been fed before I ask about the kids. As I try to fall asleep in a strange bed in a strange town, I toss and turn, worried that my wife didn't lock the doors or set the burglar alarm.

Mostly, I worry because I'm not there to watch over things.

I'm out of sorts.

My dad, if he were still alive, would have a good laugh about this. I used to have fun teasing him when he said he had to "get on home before dark." I found it amusing that a grown man—a man who served overseas in a war, worked the swing shift at the Fiberglas factory and grew his own vegetables—would put such stock in beating the sun home.

Now I understand.

Home is home. Do not disturb.

American Idol at Our House

I admit it. I am a forty-eight-year-old man who enjoys watching American Idol. Go ahead and judge. If Simon Cowell can weather the scorn heaped on him by rejected Celine Dion wannabes, then I can endure a few chuckles.

It is fascinating to watch the youth of America stand up in front of three celebrity judges (especially that meanie, Simon) and belt out the evening's tenth heartfelt rendition of "Wind Beneath My Wings." There's a lot of bravery among these kids. I never cease to be amazed by those who cannot carry a tune in a Sam's Club shopping buggy who truly believe they can sing. And when cruel Simon says, "Frankly, your voice sounds like a rabid kitty caught in the throes of an agonizing death rattle," well, you just want to cry for the poor kid, who almost always appears surprised. All his life, friends and family told him he was a wonderful singer—the next American Idol, for sure—but Simon, with one withering judgment, reduces The Next Great Thing to a puddle of despair.

What's not to love?

I also enjoy the moment when a contestant refuses to meekly accept Simon's opinion, wagging her finger in his stony face and vowing to prove him wrong by becoming the next great diva. "You'll see, Simon! I don't need you or this show. I will be a star! You'll SEE, Simon!" And with that, she and her mother, who is wearing a tee shirt with her daughter's face on it, storm out of the hall in a righteous flourish, never to be seen again ... until the same contestant shows up at the next audition with like a totally new haircut, still earnest in her belief that she has what it takes.

There's another reason I'm tuning in to American Idol this year: My daughter Amy and I enjoy it together. The first night it was on, she invited me to watch it with her, and I was hooked. We now have a standing date on Tuesday nights. It's nice to have something we do together. Such opportunities are not as limitless as they were when she was younger. We each offer running commentary as we root for the pop hopefuls, and we both make sour faces when one of them hits a bad note. We critique the singers, their clothes, their moves, the judges, even the goofy-haired host, Ryan Seacrest. I ask Amy, "What's up, dog?" in my best judge Randy Jackson impression, and she rolls her eyes and smiles. (I'm easy. I happily accept the rolling of eyes if it comes with a smile.)

Amy is a senior in high school. The sentimental, old-coot side of me is looking down the road. I'm in the countdown phase. Our house will be different when she leaves for college, just as it was when her sister left. The difference is that when Amy goes to college, there won't be a teenager in our house anymore. It's hard to remember when there wasn't a teenager running around here, leaving the lights burning—and a lingering song—to brighten every room.

But it's the way things are supposed to be. It's time for the next great adventure. When next year's season of American Idol airs, she'll likely be watching it in a dorm room with her friends. But it will be okay with me if she calls after the show to say, as judge Randy might, "I'm feelin' you, man."

Not Available in Stores

My wife would not consider herself an impulse buyer. No, the "6-Second Abs" apparatus leaning against the wall of our bedroom, she would argue, is a well-considered investment in the future—the future being whenever she decides to pick up the 6-Second Abs apparatus. It looks like a set of handlebars from a curvy futuristic black motorcycle, a sleek plastic thing that might have been teleported from the Starship Enterprise.

It works this way: You attach rubber bands of appropriate quantity and thickness, place the thing on your lap, then pull slowly until it clicks three times; then you release it—very slowly—until it clicks three more times. This exercise is supposed to give you a washboard tummy. "The yellow bands are my friends," my wife says. "The orange bands are of the devil."

The boxed set of Pilates videos she ordered was not an impulse purchase, either. She's simply waiting for the right moment to lie down on the floor and torture herself with this product. I know it is torture because I saw her and Katie taking the Pilates video for a test spin shortly after it arrived in the mail. The scene I witnessed can best be described as something resembling two turtles flipped indignantly on their backs. My wife and daughter lifted their heads off the floor and flapped their arms and legs in unison as though to will themselves airborne. I heard Katie start to laugh, then to wheeze uncontrollably, then I heard her mother chide her for not taking her health seriously. Then my wife went back to flapping.

I also am confident the Jane Fonda aerobics video was a wise purchase. This helpful product has been a trusted part of our family for several years. It is the only exercise video my wife comes back to again and again. "Time to visit Jane," she'll say when she wants to drop a couple of pounds (although I think she looks perfect, of course). She and Jane are old friends, although it wasn't that way in the early days, when one evening my wife locked herself in Amy's bedroom and started working out with Jane, only to be waylaid by The Leg Cramp from Neptune. She crawled to the door and screamed for help, which upset Amy so much that she cried herself to sleep. I definitely did not laugh at my wife that night. I definitely did not laugh a lot.

I also do not laugh so much that I almost make myself sick when she over-exercises and then sneezes and winces (like this: "Ah-choo-OWWW!"). She said this happened one day at school while she was teaching (the "Ah-choo-OWWW!" thing), and many of her young students were visibly upset, fearing that Mrs. Blume had thrown herself free of a vital organ. Impressionable young students, some of whom will throw up sympathetically at the sight of another child throwing up, don't need to hear their teacher crying "Ah-choo-OW-WW!" especially with the PACT test coming up. Life is stressful enough.

I probably shouldn't take too much delight in telling you about my wife's collection of home-exercise products. Honesty compels me to confess that I am the proud former owner of a NordicTrack Skier exercise machine, which also doubles as a trendy clothes rack.

My Favorite Things

On the road again, and the setting reminds me of our honeymoon trip nearly twenty-two years ago. We stayed in a high-rise hotel by the Atlantic Ocean. There was a telephone in the bathroom. Neither of us had seen such a thing before, so we called my wife's parents to tell them we were talking to them from a telephone in the bathroom.

I thought myself privileged for the next couple of days. (This was before the day when anyone could walk around with a telephone in his pocket.) After that first call home, we didn't have an occasion to use the telephone in the bathroom. But knowing it was there made us feel special.

Debbie and I have simple tastes. While we appreciated our nice hotel and its conveniently placed telephones, what I remember most from our honeymoon are the ordinary things. We ate dinner one night an expensive seafood restaurant, but the meal I recall more fondly was a midnight run to McDonald's. Also, one of the best cheeseburgers I ever had was at the restaurant in the hotel. The beachfront view was more than we could afford, but long after the cost of that trip faded, what I still remember is getting trapped in a traffic circle, my bride laughing as I tried to figure out how to escape.

As idyllic as our honeymoon destination was, after three days we were nevertheless ready to return home so that everybody could "see us married." We left behind the extraordinary in order to return to our ordinary life. With profound apologies to Rodgers and Hammerstein, here's my plain-folk version of "My Favorite Things," sung to the tune of the original:

> *Cubed steak and gravy and sliced red tomatoes,*
> *Laughter and stories at our supper table,*
> *Children at home, sound asleep in their dreams,*
> *These are a few of my favorite things ...*
>
> *Walking the block with my wife alongside me,*
> *Strumming my guitar the way my dad taught me,*
> *Watching a storm, sitting on my porch swing,*
> *These are a few of my favorite things ...*
>
> *When the job calls, when the world falls,*
> *When I'm feeling sad,*
> *I simply remember my favorite things,*
> *And then I don't feel so bad.*
>
> *Mowing the lawn in the new air of springtime,*
> *Watching some football on TV, come autumn,*
> *Talking with neighbors as fireflies take wing,*
> *These are a few of my favorite things ...*
>
> *Tossing a ball for my dog to chase after,*
> *Sad when a good book has reached the last chapter,*
> *Hoping for our kids, some day, families,*
> *These are a few of my favorite things ...*

When the job calls, when the world falls,
When I'm feeling sad,
I simply remember my favorite things,
And then I don't feel so bad.

My Wife Fell Out of the Car

First of all, the car was not moving. Secondly, she was not seriously hurt. Thirdly, I did not laugh for at least fifteen seconds. When I saw that she could walk, I laughed a little. Or a lot.

I should mention that this happened as we were arriving at an Episcopal church for a chamber music concert. Put the pieces together—high-brow church, classical music and a grown-up person spilling out of a car—and you've got a good story.

We were late, which was my fault because I insisted we first run by Lowe's. We pulled up near the church's entrance so I could deposit my wife before parking the van. In order to exit the vehicle, she had to step over some strips of crown moulding we'd just purchased for one of our many ongoing home-improvement projects. She negotiated the first step well enough, but when the heel of her trailing pump came down in the side pocket of the car door, all bets were off.

When you are falling, there is a moment when you realize you are falling and think you can stop it from happening. Then you are on the ground—hard—still thinking you can stop yourself from falling. This happened to my wife in the split-second between the moment she realized she was losing control of the situation and the moment the pavement made her intimate acquaintance.

From my vantage point behind the steering wheel, all I saw was a blonde blur, then a single trousered leg pointing upward at, to my estimation, was a forty-five-degree angle. I thought the sight curious, what with us being at an Episcopal church for a chamber music concert. I tried to force what I was seeing to make sense but could not. To my dawning horror, I realized that the woman I loved was on the ground.

Before I could react (Superman would have swooped in to catch Lois Lane before she hit the asphalt), I saw my wife's hand reach up and grasp the door. Then she pulled herself up and uttered something with emphasis.

"Are you all right?" I asked.

"Yes. Ow! OW!"

More emphatic utterances.

"Are you sure?"

"Yes! Just go!"

In every man's life there are key moments of decision. This was one. Was she more injured, or more embarrassed? Should I stay or ...

"GO!" she uttered.

Emphatically.

Like a guilty man fleeing a crime, I drove away and left her there. I hoped the people in the car behind me—good, decent Episcopalians, no doubt—would not judge all Baptists on the basis of my sorry behavior.

I parked as quickly as I could and joined my wife inside, where I learned that two of our daughter's friends had witnessed the unfortunate spill. Their immediate reaction—like mine—had been to flee, not wanting to bring further embarrassment to the poor falling lady. In the darkness, they failed to recognize immediately that the muttering woman on the ground was their friend's mother.

We finally took our seats, and the concert began. During the Concerto in D Major, my wife almost succumbed to a powerful urge to giggle. As for me, I was smiling, too, replaying the whole scene in my mind. If our eyes had connected at that moment, there would not have been a sufficient number of screws to hold the pew to the floor; we would have shaken it loose in an attempt to stifle our laughter.

We managed to hold everything together until the ride home, when we laughed until tears came. Then, for a mile or two, it would get quiet. Then one of us would giggle, and the whole thing would start up again. It was cleansing.

Who says classical music is boring?

Honey, I Smashed the Stove

The whole house shook when the stove slammed face-first onto the linoleum. Windows rattled. Flocks of frightened birds took flight. Squirrels suffered cardiac events. The cat, napping on a ledge outside the kitchen window, shot across the street like a starship punching into warp factor six.

It happened quickly. At 4:05:02 PM, we owned a working stove; at 4:05:04, we did not.

I stood behind the counter, slack-jawed, staring at the dusty hole where the stove had lived contentedly for fifteen years until the moment it suddenly didn't anymore. My palms were still upturned, as if the laws of physics might yet decide to return the stove to its rightful place. My wife was on the opposite side of the counter—the cataclysm side—mouth agape, eyes fixed on the ticking wreckage. Neither of us spoke. We were stunned into muteness.

Amy, who was watching television at the other end of the house, rushed to the kitchen, fearful that her father had executed a swan dive from the top of the ladder. The sight of an oven tipped forward on its face arrested even her, a teenager who is not easily impressed. There we stood, the three of us, trying to process what we were seeing. The only sound was the tinkling of glass shards dislodging themselves from the oven door and falling to the floor—that, plus an ominous unidentified dripping.

Finally, very quietly, my daughter asked, "What happened?"

"Honey," I said, "I think I killed the stove."

She looked at me, then at her mother. Then her mother looked at me. None of us knew the proper way to react in the event of a stove-killing. I started to laugh. Then they laughed, too. If Dad thought it was funny, then everything would be all right, despite the fact that I had single-handedly taken down a healthy, 200-pound kitchen appliance in the prime of its life.

While I dealt with the violent demise of our stove with calm, my wife will tell you I sometimes obsess over little things, like when my family uses their cell phones before nine o'clock at night. Maybe it's because I think I can control the little stuff. But when something big happens, I'm reminded that I'm not in control of my life. There's a certain release in knowing that. Trying to control everything is exhausting work. Worrying about phone bills wears me out. I have no strength left to worry about a dead stove.

A lot of people are more laid back than I. A friend of ours, Melanie, is that way. Raising three frighteningly active boys provides lessons about how not to sweat the small stuff. One day she drove a load of kids to school in her minivan. When one of the boys tried to close the sliding door, the whole thing came off in his hands. He literally was standing in the school parking lot holding a car door, and it wasn't even show-and-tell day. Melanie told him to throw it in the back with the loose soccer shoes and empty Burger King cups. She drove back home, enjoying a splendid open-air view.

In that same spirit, we're taking the loss of our stove in stride. Now that it's been replaced, I've noticed my wife eyeing our elderly refrigerator. It's been groaning lately. Don't be surprised if you soon hear that it has met with an unfortunate accident.

Pomp and Circumstance

A few days ago, Amy walked into the room wearing her graduation gown. Her mother burst into tears and ran upstairs.

At our house this week, and perhaps at yours, there begins a flurry of activity—academic awards ceremonies, the junior-senior prom, church recognition services, farewell speeches—all culminating at one o'clock on the afternoon of May 22, when tearful mothers' babies cross the divide and become high school graduates.

In a society that has cast off many of the old ceremonies, the rite of passage known as commencement is one we have kept intact. I wish we had more.

Last Saturday, the members of our local National Guard unit came riding into town on a parade of pride, patriotism and wailing fire engines. The rite of welcoming home war heroes dates back to ancient times. In our town, people stood along a flag-lined Main Street, waving and saluting their neighbor-soldiers, men and women who left family and home to serve—to die, perhaps—in answering the call of their country. My wife said it was like a scene in a movie. I admit, I got choked up.

It was important that those Guardsmen and -women were welcomed home in a public display—important for them, important for our community. Through such ceremonies, we remind ourselves who we are, what we value, how we are connected.

The military understands the power of ceremony. Firing a rifle volley at the funeral of a fallen warrior or ceremonially folding an American flag into a triangle—these practices speak of the bond of human experience that transcends time and history, linking the fallen soldier to all who ever died defending their country.

Several years ago, we drove to Parris Island to see a boy we'd watched grow up graduate from basic training. The day he left to join the Marines, he was Benji, a boy; the day he graduated, he was Ben, a man. He joined a band of brothers, and the pomp and circumstance that took place on the parade ground that day sealed a lifelong fraternity.

Perhaps we've tossed aside too many of the ceremonies of life. Even the high school graduate who complains about putting on a stuffy cap and gown recognizes that what he's about to do is bigger than himself.

Soon, my daughter will walk across a stage and receive a handshake and a piece of paper that validates her twelve years of schooling. But even more valuable to her than the diploma will be the people in the audience—her parents, sister and relatives, of course, but also the hundreds of people whose names she doesn't know. Their public presence, as she and her friends say goodbye to high school and embrace a brave new world, will affirm for her—and for us—her passage into adulthood.

She will be the same, but she will never be the same. And all of us will be there to bear witness.

How Time Is It?

There's been a lot of activity at our house as the calendar races toward Saturday, high school graduation day for Amy, our youngest. Invitations have been mailed, awards ceremonies have been attended, and a red graduation gown hangs in her room, pressed and ready for one final wearing.

With all of the focus on the big event, it might be easy to forget that Amy is not an only child. Her sister, Katie, a college student, has also been busy, finishing up exams and moving stuff from her dorm to an apartment she is sharing with friends, and starting a summer job.

Our children are on the home stretch toward adulthood. One could argue that Katie is already there, but I'm not ready to concede the point. Even though she will turn twenty-one this summer, I will always see her as the stuffy-nosed, sleepy-eyed three-year-old in the home movie who trundles into the den on Christmas morning, spies a package of new hair bands and says, "Santa brought me a headache."

And I will see Amy as her constant companion, tagging along after her big sister and asking, "How time is it?" Through the video camera of my mind, I see Katie playing on the swing; I see Amy playing on the swing. I see Katie move to the slide; I see Amy move to the slide. I see Katie graduate from high school; I see Amy graduate from high school. I see Katie uncovering layers of experience to discover the woman waiting to emerge; I see Amy poised to do the same.

Up to now, my daughters' lives have followed nearly identical paths. The milestones for the younger have been laid down by the elder. Because her sister blazed a trail, there was some predictability to Amy's life. That is about to change. Their paths are diverging. This fall, Amy will attend a college in a separate town from her sister.

After following in Katie's footsteps for eighteen years, Amy is setting her own course. The professors, friends, adventures, opportunities and achievements to come will be hers alone.

It is easy to feel sad, thinking about children growing in different directions. I refuse to do that. My daughters are becoming adults of their own distinct callings, but they will never stop being sisters. Their bond is unbreakable. They share a secret language, one spoken with the eyes, a code even their parents can't crack.

For me, as a parent, what happens now—as Katie trains her gaze on a closing horizon free of projects, tests and term papers, and as Amy bounds fearlessly toward the revved-up world of university life—is just as important as the early years, when I held their hands while they learned to walk. The years between high school and adulthood are an amazing journey of self-discovery. It is important for us to keep the lines of communication open. Life is not always easy, and we want them to know they are not alone.

I'm preaching to myself, I suppose. It's one thing to say the best is yet to come, but I regret that I will never again rock my children to sleep. I'm done with teaching them how to ride their bikes. I'll no longer listen with rapt attention as they describe in breathless detail the stores, school and post office that inhabit the streets of the imaginary town in our driveway.

But I will listen when they talk in breathless detail about their dorm rooms, friends, job interviews, and their hopes and dreams.

And I will marvel at how quickly time passes. How time is it? I don't know. It just is.

Nothing for My Journey

My wife loves chocolate-almond ice cream. When we happen upon a Baskin-Robbins in a new town, the discovery is no accident in her mind—it is a moment of serendipity, one of those nice surprises life offers up now and then.

Like ice cream shops, those nice surprises are just around the corner. When life starts to seem predictable and boring, something unexpected happens to reawaken the joy.

Of course, all surprises aren't joyful. Some surprises, especially those that announce themselves with a telephone call in the middle of the night, are life-altering ruptures. My dad committed suicide several years ago after being diagnosed with lung cancer. Up until he got sick, he was a man seemingly content with his life. I still haven't come to terms with how he left, and I may never. When a phone rings in the night, I am wrenched back to that awful moment.

We've all known days of profound sorrow. They are inevitable. So we seek meaning—a faith to help us wrap our minds around both the good and the bad, an acceptance that affords some sense of balance even when life swings wildly out of control. When we look back at the end of life, we hope the good times will have outweighed the bad.

It's human nature to remember the good and suppress the bad. I don't remember anything negative about my Granny Fisher, although I'm sure she had warts and worries like everyone else. I only remember her twinkling eyes, her scratchy laughter and the way she hummed and tapped her feet when she rocked. If there was sadness in my Granny Fisher, I didn't see it. Even if I had, I doubt I would remember. And when I think of my dad, it's mostly the good I remember.

There's a constant to the conversations my wife and I share when we walk around the block, or when we sit in our porch swing at twilight, or when we have a quiet supper for two at the round oak table we hand-finished in the first year of our marriage. It seldom fails that one of us, after staring for a minute out the window at the squirrels foraging in the yard, will say something about how lucky we are, how blessed to have our little family, how the good has outweighed the bad and how we wouldn't trade what we have for all the money in the world. Our experiences, good and bad, make us who we are. To borrow a phrase from the late gospel songstress Vestal Goodman, "I wouldn't take nothing for my journey now."

Kids grow up and move on with their lives. Knees wear out. Jobs are lost and found. Loved ones get sick. Telephones ring in the middle of the night. But there's a Baskin-Robbins somewhere down the road, and when we happen upon it, my wife's face will light up like a child's, and I'll know, again and always, all is well.

Beach Bum Beaver

I was on vacation, and a couple came strolling up the beach with their pet beaver. The bashful beaver was wrapped in a towel, and its "mother" cuddled it like a hairy brown baby. We gathered around and took turns petting the beaver, which, we learned, gets a bath every night. That prompted questions. How did they come to adopt a beaver? (They found her on the side of the road.) What does she eat? (She loves turnip greens.) Where does she sleep? (In the bed with them.) What is her name? (Charlene. Charlene the Beaver.) Are we on Candid Camera? (No, you are not. She is like our child. Seriously.)

We've had many pets, but not a beaver. Millie, our late golden retriever, once dragged home a dead beaver and slept with it. It was like she had her own smelly teddy bear. The next day, I hauled the beaver into the woods and buried it. Millie dug it up and slept with it again.

Millie was true to her breed: She retrieved things. In addition to the beaver, she retrieved shoes from the neighbors' carports. She once trotted up our driveway with a freshly grilled steak dangling from her chops. She came home another time toting a bag of powdered doughnuts. When she was younger, she liked to chase down rabbits. As with the beaver, she slept with the deceased rabbits. I think she was lonely.

We have a cat that likes to bring critters home, particularly flying squirrels, chipmunks and mice. She doesn't eat them. She deposits them on the doorstep. I've learned to look before I step outside. The cat (my wife calls her Puddin'; I call her Kitty) has a weird meow. The sound is all squashed up, like she's been smoking two packs a day for twenty years. When she wants to be heard, instead of "meow," it comes out more like "wrank."

"Here, kitty, kitty."

"Wrank."

We also own Gabbie, a hyped-up border collie-beagle mix. At nine years old, she's as energetic as a puppy. We got her so she could keep Millie company in her golden years. Gabbie enjoyed the job. Her favorite thing was to lick the inside of Millie's ears. If you ever looked inside Millie's ears, you would have remarked on their pink, healthy glow.

Gabbie also likes to run. And run. And run. In the tedium that is her daily existence, she lives for those exhilarating moments when neighbors pass by our yard walking their dogs. When this happens, Gabbie spins like a maniac, snatches up a shredded basketball and shakes it back and forth. Then she spins again. I don't know what message she's trying to send, but she sends it with vigor.

We've also been caretakers to a parakeet, a hamster, an aquatic frog, several fish and a few hermit crabs. The frog disappeared one day; we found him months later, a mummified, black leathery thing frozen in a permanent crouch at the back of our daughter's closet. The parakeet suffered a fatal heart attack early one morning when I flipped on the stereo. The hamster ran under the refrigerator and electrocuted himself. The fish jumped out of the tank and fell behind the bookshelf, and the hermit crabs grew antisocial and quietly slipped away.

So I mentioned the beaver story to the cat.

"Wrank."

Exactly.

Circle

All my life's a circle.

Thirty years ago, I set foot on the campus of Clemson University as a skinny, timid freshman. The biggest place I'd lived in till then was Starr, South Carolina, where the welcome sign at the edge of town read:

"Don't Blink, You'll Miss It.

"Seriously. We're Not Kidding."

The boy from the country was not ready for the big loud world of the university. A couple of years later, I transferred to a smaller college, one more suited to my introvert leanings. But I enjoyed my time at Clemson and met people who remain friends to this day.

A year or so after graduating from college, I asked out a girl I had recently met at a friend's wedding. I took her to a nice restaurant in Clemson. Then we took a moonlit stroll around the campus. The whole campus. Every single mile of rolling sidewalk. If I had said to her one more time, "Now, that's an interesting building," I'm convinced she would have come up lame. But she smiled and never complained. It was only after we were married that I learned her feet were killing her during my special walk down memory lane.

Fast-forward to today. A couple of weeks ago, we took Amy to freshman orientation at Clemson. She will be joining Tiger Nation in the fall. We spent two days either (1) sitting in meetings or (2) walking from one end of campus to the other to sit in meetings. My wife, suffering flashbacks to our first date, lobbied for us to take the bus.

I was thrilled to be my daughter's tour guide. I slipped easily into the role, pointing out my old dorm, my dining hall, my chemistry building, my favorite shady spot. Amy was too nice to say anything, but I soon came to my senses and realized the day wasn't about me. I was excited for her, even more excited than I'd been for myself all those years ago. When I told her she should soak up every moment that would be coming in the next four years, it was only because my joy for her was spilling over.

Amy's roommate this fall will be the daughter of a friend I've known since ninth grade—coincidentally, the same friend whose wedding I was at when I first caught sight of her pretty maid of honor. In less than a year the maid of honor became my wife. If that's not co-incidence enough, Amy's roommate's dad and I shared an apartment when we were students at Clemson, several years before he and my high school friend would meet and marry. How does that happen?

Life was thirty years ago. It was yesterday, and it is today. What goes around comes around, and it delights me every time.

All my life's a circle,
Sunrise and sundown.
The moon rolls through the nighttime
Till the daybreak comes around.
All my life's a circle,
I can't tell you why;
The seasons spinning round again,
The years keep rolling by. (Harry Chapin)

What We Remember

"Honey, supper's ready." Three words that evoke contentment deep and wide.

It was yesterday, about sunset. I was in the backyard, toiling in the lingering heat of a midsummer's afternoon, digging up old fence posts. The work was hard but rewarding in the way manual labor can be. I was sweating over the last of the fence posts when my wife opened the screen door and called me to supper.

Time suspended itself, and I recognized the moment for what it was: a vivid awareness of happiness. Such a crystalline instant is serendipitous. Everything is right. It comes as suddenly as a summer storm and vanishes as quickly as a doe.

But the afterglow lingered, and I knew I would invoke the moment again and again. It was a memory that would offer respite when the world would start to spin too fast again. A simple thing, standing there in my backyard and hearing my wife call me to supper, yet it was complete in a way that settled deep inside me.

We all have memories of ordinary times, episodes that stick with us for no apparent reason. Such was a time when I was six years old, exploring the field behind our house. It was a gray winter late-afternoon, and I looked up at the sky and wondered why it got dark earlier in the winter. I thought about the Lone Ranger, because I knew my favorite TV show would be coming on about the time it was getting dark. Then I heard my mother calling me in to supper, and I hoped we would be having gravy and biscuits.

Years later, when I was a college student, I was riding my bicycle along the country roads in the farming community around Pendleton and stopped on a bridge that spanned a little creek. I looked over the edge and saw a group of teenage boys and girls sitting on a sand bar in the shady coolness below, laughing and talking, doing nothing wrong. That image, as clear as a scene from a movie, has stayed with me. So will the memory of digging up old fence posts and being called to supper.

After we ate, Katie and I went for a walk. Katie is taking an astronomy course this summer, and I am her study partner. I quizzed her on the dominant molecules of the giant gas planets while we walked around town. At some point we ended up near a softball field. We sat on the bleachers and discussed the off-axis magnetic fields of Uranus and Neptune.

Later, after Katie had driven back to school and I was alone in my porch swing, I remembered another summer evening many years ago when Katie and I sat on bleachers at a ball field in another town. She was only a couple of weeks old, and I was a new dad taking my daughter out for a walk. I told her a story about a big kid named Biff who ran me over in a game of elementary school flag football. The story, or maybe my goofiness in telling it, made her smile.

Twenty-one years later, my kid and I were sitting on bleachers again, and I was saying goofy stuff to make her smile.

I'll remember that.

O, Pioneer!

I was an only child for about thirteen months. Then my sister came along, followed in short order by two brothers. Our parents worked full-time jobs, and keeping the four of us clean, fed and clothed was another full-time job. At the end of the day, there wasn't a lot of time left for parent-child bonding. Our home was happy but crowded.

I remember a time when I had my mom to myself. It happened on a summer evening in the mid-1960s, when I was ten or eleven years old. We were in the front yard, just after sunset. We lay on our backs in the grass and watched the stars come out. A bright star moved steadily across the sky. My mom told me it wasn't a star at all, but NASA's reflective radio satellite, Echo 2, and that it would move across the sky every ninety minutes or so, as predictable as the Anderson Airport beacon that swept across the western horizon. I was made witness to one of the early manmade objects to float unpowered across the heavens. Thus was ignited, like the phosphorescent tail of a Redstone rocket, my love of all things space.

A few years later, in 1972, NASA launched Pioneer 10. The plucky spacecraft studied Jupiter before it was slung outward toward the edge of our solar system. In 1983, just a few weeks before the birth of our first child, Pioneer 10 sailed past the orbit of Pluto, becoming the first manmade object to travel so far from home. On January 23, 2003, more than thirty years after it was launched, Pioneer 10 mustered enough energy from its nearly depleted power source to send a faint and final signal home. It is now a ghost ship drifting toward the red star Aldebaran (the eye of the constellation Taurus), which it will reach in two million years.

I know I romanticize these things, but the idea of a ship floating outward from its home, never to return, rings noble. The intrepid Pioneer 10 inspired me to write my first newspaper column, in which I compared the wonder of space to the mystery of looking into the eyes of my firstborn child. Today, my firstborn child is a senior in college, learning about the planets and stars in an astronomy course. As her study partner, it has been a fun experience for me—a ticket back to the night I looked up and saw Echo zip across the sky.

When Katie gets into her car to drive back to school after one of our study sessions, I wave goodbye and point to the moon—ever the tutor, reminding her to look up and see. Space, for her, is not what it was for me. But she will have a lifelong acquaintance with the night sky, and she'll be able to tell her children about the phases of the moon and explain where falling stars come from. Perhaps some summer evening she will lie on her back in the grass with her firstborn and tell the story of Pioneer 10, the spunky little explorer that could, moving ever away, out there in the night sky, its antenna pointed toward home.

Squeaky Clean

We have a noisy clothes dryer. It screeches like a tormented animal. It can be heard from outside our house. People walking past whip around to see if a rabid fox is about to attack them. A visitor in our home will hear the dryer start up and get a worried look. "Oh, that's just the dryer," we'll say and go on as if it's a perfectly normal thing.

Our dryer has done this for years. We bought it more than twenty years ago, and, despite the screech, it has never failed us. A bird once built a nest in the exhaust vent, which kept the clothes from drying, but I cleaned the nest out and everything was fine. Other than that, our dryer has operated perfectly over the course of more than 5,000 loads of laundry—except for the screech, of course, and the fact that we have to secure the door with a bungee cord if we're drying tennis shoes, which tend to kick the door open.

We've grown accustomed to the screech. Sometimes I'll walk by the laundry room and make a mental note to do something about the noise, but I never do. My daughter occasionally asks me to transfer her laundry from the washer to the dryer before I go to bed. On those nights, I fall asleep to the sound of an appliance in deep distress. I sleep like a baby.

When it comes to fixing things, I procrastinate. Take the washing machine: It walks the floor so much it should be in an Ernest Tubb song. But I live with it. Then there's the old microwave oven. The door handle broke off, but we kept using it for another fifteen years because it still popped the popcorn. In order to open the microwave, I held my hands straight out with palms facing each other (like a child does while singing the "deep" part of "Deep and Wide") then pressed against the top and bottom of the door while pulling firmly. Guests found it entertaining, but we had done it for so long we didn't even notice anymore. When we finally got a new micro-wave a few months ago, it was several weeks before I could reach for the door without assuming a martial arts posture.

There's also a wobbly doorknob I've been meaning to replace on the downstairs bathroom. I bought a new doorknob on Ebay a few years ago, but I guess I'm waiting for just the right moment to install it. Also, wallpaper is peeling in the upstairs bathroom, and I fully intend to repair the bedroom ceiling that was water-damaged when the air conditioner in the attic overflowed a couple of summers ago.

Our baby girl is leaving for college this weekend. Things will be a lot quieter around here. Maybe I'll finally get around to some of those projects. Amy's grandmother gave her some new towels to take to school with her. A couple of weeks ago her mom offered to wash them so she could go ahead and pack them. "No, thanks, Mom," she said. "I want you to wait until just before I leave, so they'll smell like they just came from our dryer."

Even as I write these words, I can hear the dryer raising a ruckus in a far corner of the house. Amy, no doubt, has been feeding it again.

Yes, things will soon be a lot quieter around here. I think I'll let the dryer be for now.

Moving Day

We moved both our daughters to college over the weekend. In the days leading up, they and their mother went shopping for essentials.

When they returned from Sam's Club, twittering like sparrows, I thought I should check their purchases. Here is what I found: 1,000 Advil capsules, 500 Aleve tablets and 1,000 Excedrin Migraine capsules.

I had no idea my children were opening a pharmacy.

"You know you can't go to Sam's and buy just one Advil," my wife said, arranging the jugs-o-pills on the counter. "If you want to buy one, you have to buy a thousand."

"Why would I want to buy one Advil?" I asked.

"Exactly," she said, and walked away, leaving me standing there with eight cans of Skintimate shaving cream, which I estimate will last two weeks.

The above-detailed cache of pain relievers doesn't begin to describe how well stocked my children are for college. Lewis and Clark were not better provisioned. In fact, the way my wife fretted about the most minute elements of our daughters' college supplies, one might think they were headed for the Oregon Trail, not towns where drug stores actually exist.

School supplies aside, the moving-in went well. In years past, moving day was hot and humid. This year the weather was nice, with temperatures in the low eighties. Both girls had rooms on the ground floor, for which my knees were sorely grateful.

We moved Katie on a Friday. The largest item we hauled was her wooden loft, which, after three years, I've become quite adept at assembling. We hauled in the television, refrigerator and bottled water and left Katie and Kellie, two weathered college veterans, to their own devices.

On Saturday morning we woke up early and started all over again. We loaded Amy's futon, clothes, shoes, photo albums and nail polish and headed up the highway in the opposite direction from the previous day. The campus was teeming with other college freshmen and anxious parents. When we finally found a place to park, a merry band of upperclassmen materialized and offered to help us unload our vehicles.

In a few hours we were done and headed home, the futon making the trip back with us because it wouldn't fit in the room. Amy's boyfriend road shotgun, and my wife, at her own insistence, sat hunched on the floor of the minivan with the upside-down futon protecting her like a teepee. Claustrophobic, she had to talk herself out of a panic attack.

After we arrived home and stowed the futon and empty boxes inside the garage, we stood in the driveway, looking for something else to do—anything to avoid going into our empty house.

"Want to rent a movie?" Debbie asked.

"Right now?"

"Right now."

"Let's go."

So off we went to the video store, where we lingered over every other title. Then we spent a casual hour in the grocery store, even though we'd both rather clean the gas grill with our fingernails than go to the grocery store.

Finally, we went home. We ate supper and put on a movie. My

wife, exhausted, was asleep before "My Big Fat Greek Wedding" was half over. She'd cheated the empty nest one more day.

Full Nest

We enter the world crying, often loudly, for what we want. Then we spend the next several years suppressing the urge to think only of our own desires. It can be a challenge, but it gets easier when children come along. We push aside thoughts of self and consider our offspring first. The child commands the stage, and everything is as it should be. It is the natural order of things.

Then we get older, and our children grow up. They spend less and less time at home, and the attachments we have formed are stretched. If we're not careful, our sadness at their leaving can turn into a full-blown pity party.

I was on the verge of printing up invitations for my pity party a few days ago. My kids are both off at college—the baby for the first time—and the house is too quiet. The screen door doesn't bang as loudly, the phone doesn't ring as often, and the ceiling doesn't thump to the rhythm of dance routines. There is less background noise from hair dryers, and the microwave doesn't ding with its announcement of a piping-hot Hot Pocket. Missing is the whrrr of a hand-me-down Honda slowing and turning into the driveway. There is not the assault of hugs when I stray into the airspace of my children.

A pity party, indeed.

Then I thought of my mom, who gave birth to me when she was seventeen and to my youngest brother when she was forty-three. In between, there were two brothers and a sister. Since the time my mother was a teenager, for forty-nine consecutive years, she has had a child living at home. My dad died a few years ago, before all the kids were grown. He and my mom never had golden years together.

Had there been an empty nest for my parents, I would have wished for them more of what they enjoyed: trips to the mountains; making music and playing cards with their friends; working in their yard; sitting in the shade under an oak tree, watching the sunset and going inside to watch some TV before bedtime; sharing a Pepsi and a hot dog after my dad got off work from the second shift; going to visit their grandchildren and returning home before dark; visiting his and her parents on Sunday afternoons; picking okra and tomatoes from Dad's vegetable garden; whispering private jokes but refusing to tell the kids what was so funny; going to the lake on a hot day; relishing a peasant's meal of cornbread and milk and sliced onion; watching Lester Flatt and Earl Scruggs and the Foggy Mountain Boys on Saturday evenings.

My parents worked hard to provide for us, but they found gleaming, enduring diamonds of happiness in the simplest things. I would have wished for them more time to enjoy the simplest things.

Their constancy in my life reminds me that my own nest will never be empty, nor will my children's, no matter how far they may go.

Angry Bees

My wife was getting ready for work when the kamikaze yellow jacket attacked her. I was asleep. Her screaming and gurgling jolted me awake. The first thing I saw after being ripped from my dream was my beloved, dancing and foaming at the mouth.

It would be a few moments before I understood that the foaming at the mouth was due to the fact that she was brushing her teeth when the attack came. Her screams, partly muffled by the frothy Crest, were the result of an angry wasp planting its stinger in her neck.

My caveman instincts kicked in. I sprang into action and headed downstairs to fetch the fly swatter. Thus, armed as David to meet Goliath, I headed into battle. The yellow jacket, drunk with victory and looking for another victim, swooped about the room and made diving runs at me, causing me to jerk, dodge and contort my limbs like a character from The Matrix. My wife, entertained, temporarily forgot her pain in the neck.

Despite being outmatched by a quicker and nastier foe, I managed, after crouching behind the ironing board and plotting—and after repeated swatting of air and walls—to slay the beast. Mission accomplished.

Or so I thought. Soon there was another, and another. Every time I dispatched one, another appeared. I thought they were coming from the air conditioner vent in the ceiling, so I sealed it over with wax paper and blue painter's tape. Very attractive, but ineffective—they were coming from elsewhere. I went back to flailing with the fly swatter, which came apart and had to be repaired with the blue painter's tape. The whole adventure was taking on a color scheme.

I finally discovered that the yellow jackets were coming from a nest they had built inside the wall of my house. From the yard, I could see them swarming about a hole near a drain pipe.

I went to the store and bought two cans of wasp spray. I trained my weapons like high-powered water guns on the hole and squeezed the triggers. Yellow jackets scattered in a cloud like fuzz off a dandelion. My surprise attack seemed to be effective, but it suddenly occurred to me that the hole on the outside of my house wasn't their only escape route. I went back inside and cautiously approached the bathroom. The whine of irate yellow jackets was audible from the hallway. My bathroom was pulsing with the collective ill humor of fifty or so highly offended yellow jackets. I crawled along the floor, shut the bathroom door and regrouped.

I drove back to the store and bought a bug bomb. I set it off in the bathroom, which took care of the yellow jacket convention but left the room smelling like an insecticide factory. I checked the hole outside and found there were still a few stubborn hangers-on. With my trusty blue painter's tape, I taped a second bug bomb to the end of a pole, pressed the release on the can and, standing there in the yard, lifted it up to the hole. I called my wife outside to see my clever invention. People driving past probably thought I was trying to paint my house with a can of Rust-Oleum taped to the end of a long stick.

In any case, it worked. No more yellow jackets. Nevertheless, for a while, we will look twice before brushing our teeth, and I am keeping a roll of blue painter's tape under the sink.

All Lit Up

I always know when my children are home for the weekend. All the lights are on.

Curling irons are plugged in a half-hour before they are needed so they can "warm up." Televisions and radios blare unattended from multiple locations. Up to three telephones ring simultaneously, while instant-messaging alerts chime impatiently from always-on laptop computers.

Long, steaming showers melt the glue from the bathroom wallpaper. Temperatures climb even higher due to the heat generated by industrial-duty hair dryers, while in the rest of the house temperatures plunge toward arctic levels because someone (a ghost named Not Me) has kicked the thermostat down another fifteen degrees.

The oven is dialed up to the perfect temperature for Pizza Bites, and a can of chicken noodle soup simmers on the stovetop. The microwave hums pleasantly before dinging its cheerful announcement of another hot and quick treat, just as our passive-aggressive toaster spits out a pair of warmed-over frozen waffles.

Upstairs, a squeaky dryer and a waltzing washing machine join forces in a laundromatic song-and-dance. I hear one of my children yell across the upstairs hallway to no one in particular: "My jeans are wrinkled. Can someone plug in the iron?"

I step out to study the electricity meter and see it is spinning like a shiny new set of slicer wheel rims. If I listen closely, I can hear the cha-ching of a tiny cash register. I sigh.

There is irony here. When I was a teenager, my dad fussed about the light bill. He trailed behind us, turning off lights and preaching that neither money nor light bulbs grow on trees. He took particular issue with my irresponsible habit of falling asleep while listening to my stereo. Sometimes it stayed on all night. This really made him mad. As a rebuttal, I calculated the cost of leaving my stereo on for eight hours, which came to about three and a half cents. My dad was not at all impressed with my mathematics skills. In fact, he said I was being a smart aleck, which I didn't think I was. But I probably would call my kid a smart aleck if she did the same thing. Time has a way of altering one's perspective.

There's more than just an uptick in kilowatt usage when my daughters come home for the weekend. There's noise: the noise of high heels clicking on stairs … of chatter at the kitchen counter while Mom pulls together the fixings for her daughters' favorite chicken-and-rice dish … of piano music floating from the living room as Katie works on a new song … of Amy singing to the cat through the kitchen window.

There is also laughter. When the four of us are together, laughs inevitably erupt at the dinner table. It's easy laughter that comes from being with those who know you best but love you anyway.

The smiles my children bring home with them shine light in every dim corner of this old house. I always know when my girls are home for the weekend. The place is all lit up.

Friday Night, No Plans

With no particular plans on a Friday night, my wife and I ended up at a cozy roadside steak house just outside Belton. It was crowded, so the proprietor took our name and told us we could wait in our car. He would come for us when our table was ready.

He told several other folks the same thing, so as the people inside the restaurant enjoyed their baked potatoes and medium-wells, a community of us, the hungry-but-patient, waited in the parking lot and kept our heaters cranked up against the February chill. It was really very comfortable—much more so than standing and waiting just inside the crowded, drafty entrance.

Every few minutes, the man—a slim, smiling, fidgety fellow—bounded out the front door, scanned the parking lot, spied the next party and waved them in. After thirty minutes, we were the happy recipients of the coveted wave.

We were seated, and a polite young waiter appeared, ready to take our order. Our salads arrived quickly, and before I could reach for my second pack of Captain's Wafers, our meals were placed before us. I had the ribeye, medium. My wife had the fried flounder. The food was delicious. We left with contented tummies, and the hit on my wallet wasn't all that bad, especially considering the value-added curbside service.

That would have been a good enough night, but it wasn't over. After supper, we decided to visit my wife's parents. Our daughter Katie and her date were there, so the six of us congregated in the den. As they usually do, Debbie and Katie began serving up commentary on some of the hundreds of family photos that cover the walls and adorn the tops of end-tables, the television, bookshelves, the mantle and the hearth. My wife's parents' den is a living history museum, with a birth-to-present bragging gallery for each of their five grand-children. There also are photos of my wife and her sister, including one of a teenage Debbie sporting straight, center-parted seventies hair and striking a spunky, high-stepping pose in her majorette uni-form. For years, our children have taken unusual delight in pointing out that photo to their friends. ("Nice legs, Mom!") There's also a photo of Debbie's sister from her Glamour Shots period. I can't begin to describe the affluence of hair. To be fair, I appear in some of the photos, too, and the words "geeky" and "smirky" (and other Seven Dwarfs-sounding names) come to mind when I see myself looking down from the wall of fame.

From the comfort of my mother-in-law's glider-rocker, I smiled as Debbie and Katie took turns entertaining us with their takes on the family gallery. I saw the tension of a long week melt away from my wife's shoulders. This usually happens when we visit her par-ents; for the brief time we are there, she allows herself the luxury of being a child again, of temporarily letting someone else take up the worrisome stuff of life. It was something to see. She lay her head on a pillow in her dad's lap. Without a word, he began gently scratching her back. The years slipped quietly out the door, and suddenly there was the smiling girl with the peaceful eyes I'd first met in this same room more than twenty years before.

The best moments are the ones we don't plan.

Looking for Mr. Squiggles

Mr. Danté Squiggles. That's what my wife wanted to call the puppy if it was a boy.

When I told her a boy puppy would spend most of his waking hours chewing furniture and marking his territory, she said she wanted a girl puppy. I have no idea what she might call a girl puppy, although she's probably picked out an adorable name, something that sounds like a fabric softener.

All this puppy talk started as a passing comment, something said in the quiet of evening by a mother who was missing her children. After spending twenty-one years raising our daughters, she suddenly found herself childless when the youngest went away to college. She missed the after-school times with Amy, when the slanted rays of afternoon light warmed the sunroom as they sat on the old slip-covered couch and watched Oprah and talked about their days.

That's what she was experiencing when she said, "I want a puppy."

"You do not want a puppy," I said. "We already have two dogs and a cat."

"But they live outside. I want a little indoor dog."

"You don't want an indoor dog."

"I want to come home and have something get excited and bark and wag its tail and sit in my lap while I watch Oprah."

"I can do that."

"You're not funny, and you're not furry."

I listed the responsibilities that come with an indoor dog: the training, the crying, finding someone to take care of it when we were out of town. She agreed it wasn't a good idea. I thought the notion would pass.

And it might have passed if I hadn't mentioned it to a coworker. She has a little house dog, a Bichon Frisé named Snickers. I went to the Internet to try to find a picture of my coworker's breed. I Googled "little house dog." A photo of a Maltipoo (half Maltese, half poodle) popped up. It was adorable. In a moment of cuteness-induced insanity, I emailed the photo to Debbie. She fell in love. It was all over. I had done myself in.

Debbie has been on a quest ever since. We went to pet stores, but none had Maltipoos. She heard that Maltipoos might be available at the Jockey Lot, so we went there on a Saturday morning. We walked up and down Puppy Alley. My wife ran ahead of me, hurrying from one vendor to the next like a desperate mother in an I Want My Baby Back Lifetime movie. There were no Maltipoos. She left depressed. I, however, found a replacement knob for the gear shift on my Snapper mower, so I felt pretty good about the morning.

Debbie came home and started doing her own research. She now has her name on several Maltipoo waiting lists. It's just a matter of time before we have an addition to our family.

I went outside to break the news to Millie, our golden retriever, and Gabbie, our six-year-old hyperbolic beagle-border collie mix. Millie, who has been with us more than fourteen years and has seen some ups and downs, took the news in stride. Gabbie, our nervous pet, didn't hear anything I said. All she saw was the cat behind me. ("Here comes the cat ... I'm not bothered by that ... cat ... still ... coming ... I'm calm ... cat looking at me ... CAT!CAT!CAT!")

All that dog needs is one more thing.

Peripheral Vision

I like to polish off an afternoon of yard work by relaxing on my porch swing and watching the twilight drift down and settle over my neighborhood. The first moment I'm in the swing is the purest: the instant when the anticipation of the experience meets the commencement of the experience. Then the minutes pass, and although it's still pleasant, the anticipation that drew me to my swing has been consumed in the act of sitting there. The moment, like a supernova, came into being and instantly began to be gone.

The first taste of watermelon is the sweetest, the first rumblings of a thunderstorm the most exciting. It's that way with much of the good stuff of living: the anticipation of Christmas morning, the tantalizing aroma of fried chicken drifting across the yard from a neighbor's kitchen, the first sighting of longed-for snow. Everything leads up to a moment, then the moment happens, then it starts to fade.

There is an idea that suggests that the mystery of the thing we desire is lost the very moment we possess it. We need mystery. In our attempt to demystify life, we lose sight of that which we desire (which is the desire itself). Likewise, a physicist who studies quantum mechanics will tell us that no event can be observed at the subatomic level without the observing of it altering the event itself. By seeing it, we change it.

Illumination is a point, a singular moment. Our human nature makes us want to stretch the point into a continuous line. Yet it is a point, unyielding. In our memory or imagination it may seem to be more than a point, but in remembering something, or imagining something, we're really just returning again and again to a point, a singular moment of comprehension.

Have you ever looked up into a cold night sky and stared at a constellation, only to become aware of a dim star beginning to appear in your peripheral vision, but when you shifted your gaze and tried to focus on the dim star, it disappeared? This is because the millions of light receptors in our eyes, called rods, are highly concentrated in our peripheral vision. To see a very dim star—to sense it, really—we literally have to look at it sideways. However, human nature being what it is, we will again try to look directly at it, and it vanishes. It can be maddening.

And so it is with sitting in my porch swing, or broadcasting fertilizer over my yard, or hugging my children before they drive away, or throwing a tennis ball for my dog to chase, or filling the bird feeder, or making my wife a cup of evening coffee, or locking up the house at midnight and gazing out the window into the dark.

I see it all quite clearly, and in the corner of my eye, I sense God shining.

Some Things Never Change

My wife and I were at Cracker Barrel, waiting for our soup and cornbread to materialize from the kitchen. We fiddled with our iced-tea glasses and talked about what we always talk about: our children. I don't remember what our conversations were about before we had children.

We realize this could be a problem for us as our children move on and start their own families, so we've tried to train ourselves to discuss other subjects. My wife, an elementary school music teacher, can tell some entertaining stories about the things her students say and do (much of which I am not at liberty to repeat). Then she might follow with an impassioned soliloquy about the need for medicated shampoo for the dog. For my part, I might offer up a layman's commentary on the therapeutic benefits of root beer served in a frosted mug, and I can wax poetic on the apple-butter-and-biscuit experience.

Still, no matter what subject we start out discussing, we usually make our way around the bend and end up where we started: talking about the kids. We are first, and always, parents. Some things never change.

When we arrived at the restaurant, we bumped into Miss Mary Lou, a wonderful person who taught both our children in preschool. She and her husband said they were looking forward to the birth of their third grandchild. They said the experience of having grandchildren was even more wonderful than having children. They beamed while talking about their grandchildren. They showed pictures. Listening and watching, I began to understand that we parents make a seamless transition from talking about our children to talking about our grandchildren.

Our food arrived. As we ate, I looked around the restaurant. At a nearby table was a young family—a dad and mom and two young daughters. The girls looked to be about eight or nine, and the way they never stopped talking, never stopped moving, I was reminded of what our family looked like only a few years ago.

When our girls were young, we sometimes left them in the care of their grandparents while we stole away for dinner and a movie. Even then, when a quiet meal for the two of us was something exceedingly rare—we always ended up talking about our children. Some things never change.

Not long ago, our daughters rode with us in the minivan to visit friends for dinner. The opportunities for the four of us to ride together are increasingly rare. On the way, they gabbed and giggled and picked at each other. On the ride home, they tipped their seats back and slept with their mouths open. Some things never change.

When we got home, they drove away in their own cars in different directions. Later, both called to let us know they had arrived safely at their homes away from home. We still insist on that. "Call us when you're leaving, and call us when you get there. Just call. Oh, and don't forget to call." Some things never change.

Later, we lay in bed and watched the weather, and we talked some more about the girls. I turned out the light and closed my eyes. Sleep stole in as twilight from beyond the horizon of my thoughts, and my children, like summer lightning, flashed across my fading consciousness.

Old Bird

I am turning into an old man. The signs are there. They are most recognizable to my children, who possess highly developed old-coot-detecting antennae. But some of the signs are apparent even to me: fretting over gasoline prices, having nightmares about the crabgrass invading my yard, bragging that I have shoes older than my children, or making corny jokes in an attempt to be clever in front of my kids' friends.

In addition to all that, I have taken to bird-watching, clearly an old person's hobby. I don't know of any young person who sits and watches birds unless he is being taught a valuable lesson. (I did meet a graduate student last summer who was charting the territory of a particular songbird, but he was doing it for the shamefully impure motive of getting an A in his class.) Nowadays, when my children come home from college to visit (or to wash clothes, or to loiter in the general vicinity of my wallet in case twenty-dollar bills flutter like homing pigeons into their pockets), they are likely to enter the back door and find me crouched against the opposite wall, peeking over the windowsill.

"Shhh!" I say. "Come over here—slowly!—and see this. There are five male cardinals, and their mates are fighting each other. This is cool!" My children eye each other with only slightly concerned expressions.

The squirrels are driving me nuts. (Get it? Driving me nuts? This is exactly the kind of clever thing I might say in front of my kids' friends.) All I want to do is feed the birds and watch them enjoy themselves while I have my morning coffee, but those squirrels are determined to ruin everything.

First, I tried hanging my bird feeders using cotton twine; the squirrels gnawed through it. Next, I turned to vinyl-sheathed wire clothesline; they wrapped their little rodent fingers around it and shimmied down to the feeder. Next, I used bare metal wire, too thin for their squirrelly little fingers; no problem—they leapt from the tree trunk to the feeders like maniacal trapeze artists. They knocked down my finch feeder, chewed a hole in the side and gorged themselves. The finches, to their credit, gave the squirrels a serious chirp-lashing.

There's also the issue of how to store the bird seed. I thought it would be safe inside a heavy-duty Tupperware container. Wrong. The gray bandits sniffed it out in less than twenty-four hours and chewed a baseball-size hole through the top and attempted to yank a ten-pound bag of sunflower seeds through the opening.

But I am not giving up. Stubbornness is another sign of old age. I can match wits with any simple-minded rodent. My wife will confirm this.

Sweet Millie

The first time my children saw Millie, she was a bounding bundle of fur. Katie was seven, Amy was about to turn five, and a three-month-old golden retriever puppy was about to become the newest member of our family.

The whole event is captured on an aging VHS tape. It was a foggy morning. The girls had no idea where we were going. A child's trust in her parents is a tender thing to behold. They were chattering about their school Christmas parties when we pulled into an unfamiliar driveway.

The man who lived there greeted us, and at his side was an inquisitive puppy. Her tail swished the air, and she chased every scent in the yard. Our children didn't suspect a thing, even as they warmed to this delightful creature that seemed content to lick their hands until the end of time. When we told them the dog would be coming home with us, it was several minutes before the reality sank in.

We named her on the drive home. Someone suggested Brandi. Then another offered Millie, and it stuck. "I know how to spell it," said Katie, "M-I-L-L-I-E!"

"Millie Ginger Blume!"

"Miss Millie!" squealed my wife, who attempted to videotape the ride home. There are several shots of the ceiling of our minivan, and there's a disturbing close-up of my wife's eye that was preserved for perpetuity when she became confused about which end of the camera was the viewfinder.

In no time, Millie became a member of our family with full privileges. During the day, while we were at work and school, she explored the woods, creeks and carports of our neighborhood. She brought home souvenirs: a solitary shoe, a bag of powdered donuts, a freshly grilled rib-eye steak, a deceased beaver. When we were home, she stationed herself by the back door, always at the ready in case one of us should require unconditional love. She waited for hours for the opportunity to love one of us if only for a few seconds. "Sweet Millie," my wife began calling her.

Last week, the time came to let Millie go. It had been years since she ran through the woods, and she was too feeble to stand on her own. But the sweetness was still there, in her eyes. With our hearts breaking, we lifted her onto the bed of the pickup truck. She loved to ride. We drove to the vet's office, where the doctor met us in the parking lot and told us, in the kindest way, what we already knew. We cried and said our goodbyes. I cradled Millie's head; she took a couple of deep breaths, and then she slipped away.

We called the girls. Together, as a family, we buried Millie in the shade of a dogwood tree, just a few feet from where she lived the final years of her life.

On a misty December morning fourteen years ago, when we first welcomed Millie into our family, our youngest child saw fit to announce: "Now we've got five people." She was right. Millie was one of us. Happy trails, sweet girl.

Big Plans

Every Friday morning, a cheery coworker appears in my doorway and inquires: "Do you have Big Plans for the weekend?"

My palms start to sweat. I shift nervously. I feel like I did in fifth grade when Mrs. Jones called on me to define "hypotenuse." Now, as then, I fear giving the wrong answer. (For the record: "A type of tenuse" is not the correct answer.)

Why am I uncomfortable? Why do I try to come up with an answer that will sound impressive? The truth is, we simply are not Big Plans people. Life is too busy, and we view weekends as an opportunity not to Plan anything Big. We prefer to keep our weekends free to … well, do something Big if we feel so moved. However, we usually don't feel so moved, and we're content just to hang around and do little things, such as eat things that are not healthy and maybe talk about doing some Big Things.

Not that we haven't been doing things. We spent the better part of the summer painting several rooms in our house. My wife and I consider that a Big Job. (Just picking a paint color can be exhausting. We finally settled on "Buckhead Hills." Our dining room is now a pleasant shade of subdivision.) When I was a young man, I thought nothing of coming home from work at the end of the day and spending the next several hours pounding nails into a deck. While my body has aged, my optimism hasn't; my brain believes I can still do the things I did when I was thirty. I tackle new projects with the full intention of logging a couple of hours of home-improvement time each evening. The plan sounds good on paper, but the very act of eating supper tires me out.

So most of the work falls to Saturday. We go to sleep Friday night with the earnest intention of waking up early and toiling all day. But when we finally get up (it is Saturday, after all), there's a sugary breakfast and a long, drawn-out cup of coffee. It's just wrong to rush a Saturday morning cup of coffee. We usually get moving around ten-thirty. Before we know it, it's lunch time, which we follow up with rest and, perhaps, a check of what's on TV. We finally get back to work, where, in no time, we both start hinting that perhaps we should call it a day:

"We sure have been working hard today."

"Yes, we have. I feel good about what we've accomplished."

"We shouldn't push ourselves to exhaustion. We'll only get frustrated."

"You're probably right. Are you feeling a milkshake?"

And so, another weekend … another dent in the Big Job. As rewarding as it feels, it probably wasn't what my coworker had in mind when she inquired about my Big Plans:

"So you're still painting?" she asked.

"Yes … still painting."

"And is this a new project?"

"Uh … no. Same one."

"Oh. [Insert: awkward silence.] Well, on Saturday we're going to drive all morning to another state and spend the afternoon walking along several miles of trails through some lovely botanical gardens. Then on Sunday afternoon we'll attend a financial-planning seminar so we can learn how to live comfortably in our golden years."

"Besides painting," I respond, "we'll probably get chili-cheeseburgers and onion rings from the Clock and watch the Gaither Homecoming Hour."

"That sounds like fun."

"We enjoy it."

Moving Day Again

Last week we moved our baby girl back to college for the start of her senior year. I find it hard to believe that this child, who was a bubbly middle school cheerleader only last week, will soon be looking for a job and thinking about health insurance.

This is her fourth moving season, and each year she has chosen to live in a new place. She has accumulated a lot of stuff. Some of it has not survived her evolving sense of decor, and now it resides in our garage, awaiting a second shot at life at some future yard sale. (On occasion, we sit around the supper table and foresee this mythical yard sale. We imagine that when we advertise the event—my wife calls it the "Big Old Yard Sale"—hordes of bargain-hunters will descend to rid us of our dusty accumulation, making us rich in the process.)

Moving day requires that I be available to do daddy stuff, such as lashing a bulky headboard (which Amy and I created in an afternoon of HGTV-inspired handicraft) to the luggage rack of the minivan. This is exactly the kind of task for which I claim absolute authority. I take pride in my ability to pack things into trunks and tie things to roofs of automobiles. I don't know where the urge to be in charge of strapping down the vehicle comes from, but it is a man thing. Notwithstanding the fact that we're forced to pull over to the side of the road because the headboard attempts to take wing like an upholstered beige stealth fighter, we eventually, at a steady thirty-five miles per hour, make it to Amy's newest temporary home.

As much as I gripe about the heat (and moving days are always sweltering), and even if I complain because I forgot to bring the right tools, my daughter gives a little smile, and I know she knows that I'm not really upset. It's just the role I play. We both realize that moving day is a rite of passage—for her as well as for us. We know the day will pass too quickly, that we will find ourselves missing a part of our lives that never will come again.

It is an observation made by just about everyone: Life goes by too fast. I've rebelled at the idea, wanting to believe that if I pay close attention, life will slow down. I must have looked away for the briefest moment, however, because now she's grown. It was like staring at the short hand of the clock—I didn't see it moving, even though it was always moving.

My children went from preschool to graduate school in a moment. I acknowledge the passage of time, and I clearly see they are no longer little girls. With bright minds and big dreams, they are far ahead of where I was at that age. But it still feels as though my children are six and eight, and we are hiking through the woods behind our house, stopping to eat sandwiches on a rock beside the creek. Or they are in the kitchen, flour drifting from their hair, helping their mom make biscuits.

Like moving day, those are the times I want to keep, the hands of the clock I want to freeze.

Little General

Be careful what you say, for God has a sense of humor. I said we would never have a little yappy dog. We have a little yappy dog.

By definition, a little yappy dog looks for any excuse to pitch a hissy-fit. That describes Napoleon, our twenty-pound, fluffy white, half-Maltese, half-poodle. If he hears the back door opening, he pounces atop my wife (a chivalrous maneuver designed to impress her) and goes berserk. It doesn't matter that the back door is not really opening; it is only necessary that the dog, for no apparent reason, suddenly is stricken by the thought that the back door could be opening. That is reason enough for him to leap from the end of the couch onto my wife's belly, knocking the breath out of her while he commences to barking insanely. In the presence of such heroism, worrying about a hernia or ruptured eardrum seems ungrateful.

Napoleon is not our family's first dog, even if he is the most urgently vocal. First came Millie, a gentle golden retriever who lived with us for fourteen years. She was a puppy and our girls were young when we adopted her. Millie was a faithful companion to our children, trotting alongside them in the driveway during the years of tricycles, bicycles and, finally, automobiles. "Sweet Millie," we called her, because she was.

When Millie was older, my wife and children came home one evening with a puppy—because Millie was "lonely" and needed a "friend." After a few unsettled weeks, a disgruntled Millie finally resigned herself to the fact that this impudent upstart, whom we called Gabbie, wasn't going away. Gabbie, a black-and-white beagle-border collie mix, adored Millie. We would look out the window to discover Gabbie grooming her adopted sister, a procedure Millie learned to tolerate and eventually, I believe, to appreciate. Gabbie's purpose in life was to keep Millie's ears squeaky clean. Millie died two years ago, but we still have Gabbie, who spends her days patrolling her corner of the backyard (exhibiting righteous indignation whenever Napoleon's nature calls violate her jurisdiction), napping, and dreaming of bolting across open pastures.

If you don't count parakeets, hamsters and hermit crabs, Napoleon is our first real indoor pet. When I was growing up, our dogs stayed outside. When my wife was growing up, her dog, a brittlely neurotic chihuahua named Sissy, lived inside. Like Napoleon, Sissy barked when she imagined someone might be lurking at the back door. Naturally, when Debbie and I made the decision to replenish our empty nest with a puppy but disagreed over whether the dog should live inside, we compromised: The dog would live inside.

For all his bravado, Napoleon can be a lot of fun. In some ways he is the boy I never had. He wrestles with me. He chases golf balls in my backyard. He follows me around the house. He howls when I do my fire siren imitation. When I come home from work at the end of the day, he lavishes me with such affection that I feel guilty for not spending more time with him.

Still, he is a momma's boy. If forced to choose between her and me, unless there is food involved, he chooses her. She cuddles him, talks baby-talk to him and dresses him in special outfits for every occasion, including Halloween and Clemson football games. He has his own jersey.

When it's time for me to take him for a walk, he buries his face in the cushions of the couch, an escape tactic my wife encourages. When I finally manage to corral him and we set off around the block, he ranges ahead, nose to the ground, inhaling the rich aroma of life.

Little yappy dog, little happy dog.

Jesus Tree

We were looking out the window, lamenting the damage wrought by relentless drought. Dead needles from a cedar tree formed a brittle brown blanket on the ground beneath its branches. The grass in our yard had long since been reduced to little more than dusty stubble.

Yet the pink blossoms of an optimistic crepe myrtle tree bobbed in the breeze and brushed against the window. My wife was the first to notice. It is a grand old crepe myrtle, perhaps twenty feet tall, and its limbs intertwine elegantly in a lifelong dance with an elderly dogwood. Debbie said she has always liked the smooth bark of a crepe myrtle. She said she used to call it a "Jesus tree," probably because its twisting, gnarly trunk reminded her of the trees she saw in Bible-story books when she was a child.

"Jesus tree." What a delightful expression, one I had never heard from her, even though she and I have been living together more than twenty-five years. One moment we're enjoying a cup of coffee on a Saturday morning, then she utters the words, "Jesus tree," and, like a portal in the blue September sky, a window opens onto my wife's spirit. I imagine a quiet young girl dangling from a crepe myrtle and, drawing from what she has learned of life, deciding it must be a Jesus tree. In the time it takes me to sip from my coffee mug, my appreciation for what I don't know about my wife grows a hundredfold. What else don't I know?

Here's what most people do know about her:

She is a teacher who demands the best from her students, and they give it to her because they know she loves them. She is a pianist whose music brings tears to listeners. She is a Clemson football fanatic who drives her dog to a nervous breakdown with the random shrieks she directs at the TV. She likes to get up a group of people to go out to Cracker Barrel, and she loves to exchange stories about funny things that happened at church because you're not supposed to laugh in church.

And here's what I know about her that most people don't:

She enjoys stomping on dry acorns because of the satisfying pop they make when they explode. Sometimes nothing but a chocolate-almond ice cream from Baskin-Robbins will satisfy her. She thinks about her children more than they think about themselves, and she prays for them even when they don't know they need praying for. She can write her name using either hand. She despairs when something bad happens to one of her students. She is convinced baby Cokes taste better than regular Cokes. She makes chicken casserole just for her girls, and she makes cubed steak and rice and gravy just for me. She relishes the smell of fresh two-by-fours. She has a laughing fit every time the Griswold family station wagon goes airborne in the Christmas Vacation movie.

And now something to add to these. For the rest of my life, every time I see a crepe myrtle, an echo will come back to me, borne on a morning summer breeze and sounding like her:

"Jesus tree."

Rescuing the Family History

I've recently thrown myself into an ambitious project: converting our family movies from tape to DVD. It's a real archeological dig, a painstaking unearthing of lost events. Whenever I slip an unmarked tape into the VCR and press PLAY, it's like prying open a cobweb-en-shrouded treasure chest.

No one else seems all that excited. Apparently I am the only one worried about the prospect of losing four continuous hours of tape of my three-year-old daughter, squealing and running back and forth between the beach umbrella and the ocean's edge. Over and over. Many times. Again and again. Squealing.

Undeterred, and for the sake of historical preservation, I offer some artifacts I have reclaimed for my children and future generations:

• The Hokey Pokey. I didn't know "The Hokey Pokey" had so many verses. Neither did I remember that there are exceedingly numerous body parts that can be put in, put out, then shaken all about. What I do know is this: I have it on tape.

• The amusement park at the Myrtle Beach Pavilion. If we have one video of our children and their cousins going around in circles on a boat ride and clanging a bell, we have ten. Circle ... clang ... circle ... clang. Clang, clang, clang. The eardrum-splitting clarity of the bell, even on twenty-year-old (Clang!) videotape, is astounding. Pass the Excedrin (Clang!) Migraine, please.

• Fashion statements: Braces, big "Belton bangs," humongous

eyeglasses with designer Smurf frames, dresses with puffy shoulders, Sam & Libby shoes, glitter-painted sweatshirts. I could go on.

- Ambush shots: Sneaking up on Minnie Ruth, my wife's mother, and getting a medical-quality close-up of her ear, followed immediately by a shriek and her attempt to escape by cowering.

- Puppycam: A ranging exploration of the front yard from a dog's eye view—complete with barking, sniffing, leg-lifting and chasing a fleeing toddler.

- The Moammar Kadafi bombing run. This one requires explanation. What was supposed to look like a fighter-jet cockpit view of a bombing run, swooping low over the Mediterranean and banking left to deposit lethal ordnance on the Libyan strongman's desert hideaway, turned out more like this:

ME: Ready?

SHAWN: (hoisting the clunky, early-1980s video cassette recorder in its padded bag over one shoulder and the separate ten-pound battery over the other, checking to make sure that cables between his equipment and the camera, which I am carrying, are secure) Ready!

ME: Go! (Lurching shots of ocean foam slipping away beneath us ... sounds of two grown men high-stepping through the surf: splash! splash! splash! ... in the frame, shadows clearly visible of two swimsuit-clad goofballs, running, apparently connected by wires, struggling to avoid dropping expensive equipment they do not own into the Atlantic Ocean ... jet-engine afterburner sound effects ... video signal breaking up when two idiots slam into each other then bounce apart and jerk the connecting cables halfway loose ... the sound of giggles unbecoming a fighter pilot … people staring, instinctively pulling their children close … banking left.)

SHAWN: Bombs away! (My young daughter Katie and her grandfather, bizarrely out of context, standing next to Kadafi's hideaway … wet sand bombs sluicing through the air and splattering against the sandcastle … explosion sound effects.)

We shot the scene four times, just to make sure we got it right. I don't want to brag, but I think we nailed it.

In most of our family movies, you won't see me; I'm usually the one behind the camera. My favorite recorded moments are the ones where my children unselfconsciously address me through the lens, telling me what happened at school or describing what it means to be four years old. (It means she intends to sleep all by herself, even if she is a "little bit" scared.)

Lost conversation, found treasure.

Play

My walk at lunchtime takes me past a playground full of preschoolers. The sounds and sights of play—seekers counting to ten before, ready or not, they go in search of the hiders … girls singing and swinging … boys yelling and sprinting in a rowdy kickball contest—tap a dormant wellspring of joy for the simple acts of running, jumping and shouting. I smile and continue on my way, my blood pressure perceptibly lower.

Our daughters, both grown, have told me that many of their favorite memories are of playtime. The times I spent playing with them—wrestling on the floor, jumping on the trampoline, swinging them across the creek as they clung to a rope, or dragging them around the yard in a cardboard box—are my favorite memories, too. When I pass the playground and hear the simple sounds of happy children, I can still hear my own children calling out, "Daddy, watch me!" as they cut cartwheels in the yard.

Amy, our youngest, is a senior in college. These days she is occupied with finishing strong and finding a good job after graduation. She is a disciplined student, and even though we have cautioned her against overextending herself, she works two part-time jobs—one because she loves it, the other because it's a foot in the door for a possible career. But with her self-discipline, she still knows how to play. At twenty-one, she manages to strike a balance that some of us who are older and supposedly wiser have trouble doing.

If I sometimes think she's leaning too far toward being a Responsible Adult, it's because I don't want her to lose touch with her inner child. When she was little, her days were lived at full tilt, and when I rocked her to sleep at bedtime, she often drifted off in mid-sentence while recounting in breathless detail the things that happened to her during the day. There were no wasted opportunities, especially in her moments of play. I sometimes worry that life may become too demanding of her. But she is resilient. My bets are on her.

Returning from lunch, I pass the playground. The children are gone. I spy a red ball, an escapee from the kickball game, resting next to the curb. I pick it up and run my fingers over the familiar textured surface. The sounds and smells of a thousand recesses rush forth. I step forward to drop the ball over the fence, then pause. I look around to make sure no one is watching. I lean back and fling the ball high into the air and follow the arc of its ascension, its arrest at apogee, and its satisfying plunge toward the sand on the other side. As the ball bounces over the monkey bars, I turn and walk toward work, ready to face whatever awaits.

The Ring

A few weeks ago we attended a ring presentation ceremony for Amy, who is a senior at Clemson University. It was a pleasant event, held on a late summer's evening at the university's open-air Owen Pavilion, which is like the world's biggest picnic shelter.

Parents and siblings were present in abundance, as were digital cameras. Those of us who have witnessed every significant event of our children's lives through the lens of a camcorder found ourselves at it once again. Perhaps we sensed the ticking of a giant invisible clock marking the slipping-away of days. We busied ourselves with attempting to capture and lock away another important moment in our children's lives.

I know this is a recurring theme, this anxiety I feel over the empty nest. But what else would I be thinking about? This happens to be our life right now. A few years ago I was fretting over braces and driving lessons. The circle keeps turning, and here I am.

Truth is, as with most of the things I lose sleep over, I shouldn't worry. In the year since our older daughter married, we have found ourselves wandering around our empty nest, and—guess what?—it ain't that bad. Now that it's just the two of us, a quieter, comfortable pace has eased into our days. (There's still the matter of an attention-starved little dog, but we're all adjusting.) Our children have been in our home for most of our marriage; now we're discovering that everyday life consists mainly of just us.

No more piano lessons, cheerleading practices, dance competitions, twice-a-week allergy shots, birthday parties at McDonalds, or escorting my girls onto the football field at their high school homecomings. I no longer follow my children through the house turning off lights they've left on. The place is so quiet that even the little dog imagines he hears things, which makes him all the more jittery.

My kids may no longer be home, but their energy is. Their life force is strong; its afterglow lingers wherever they have been. I walk by their rooms, and even though I know they aren't there—studying, painting their nails or talking on the phone—it feels so possible that they could be that I catch myself turning to look. Their addresses have changed, but they still live where they always will: in our hearts. They continue to have busy lives, but they no longer require their parents' daily involvement. And that's okay. It's the way it should be.

As for us, we're finding that we look forward to the quiet at the end of the day. Whether we drive to the next town for a fish supper, take a walk, sit in the swing, or talk about the kids over a cup of coffee, we are catching glimpses of a new kind of life. The door we are walking through these days holds no less promise than the one we passed through the day we got married.

In the few minutes before my daughter's ring ceremony begins, my son-in-law and I slip away to the adjacent golf course for a look at the seventeenth green, the famed "Tiger Paw." Then we stroll to the eighteenth tee and discuss where to hit our imaginary drives, which we both nail. We make our way back to the ceremony, where I sit and watch, thankful for the past, the present and the future.

Cars We've Loved

In 1981, when I went on the first date with the girl I would talk into marrying me, my chariot of choice was a 1973 Ford LTD Brougham. I didn't know what a brougham was, but I thought it sounded impressive enough to include as part of the full name when telling anyone what I drove: "A 1973 Ford LTD." (Pause.) "Brougham."

The car was a parade float with 400 cubic inches of V-8 get-up-and-go, low to the ground, with separate time zones for each bumper. It was the only full-sized automobile I'd ever coveted. My dad went with me to the used car lot and was impressive in talking the dealer down to $2,000. My payments were seventy-five dollars a month. It was "fully loaded," which was something I enjoyed hearing myself say almost as much as "Brougham."

I wanted to impress my date, so I washed, Windexed and buffed the Brougham to a military gleam. The only thing not perfect was the electric-powered window on the passenger side, which, if activated, would slide down into the door and disappear, like a chipmunk down a hole, never to emerge again. As we backed out of her parents' driveway, the first words I uttered to the woman I would ask to become my spouse were, "You probably don't want to touch that door." Looking back, I can see how she might have taken it the wrong way.

By sheer luck, I managed to talk her into a second date, and I found her sympathetic to the Brougham's qualities. That's because she, too, drove a big old car, a hand-me-down early-1970s Buick LeSabre with a Turbo Hydra-Matic transmission. It was navy with a white vinyl top, and, like my titanic Brougham, the kind of behemoth you would park in the middle of the road to block a zombie invasion.

And so it was that we brought to our marriage a dual set of gas-guzzling, possum-squashin', cruise-controlled supertankers on wheels. We affectionately named them Felicia Ford and Betsy Buick—our first two girls. Our vehicles weighed more than our apartment, but they were paid for. That changed when we purchased our first car together—a red, two-door 1981 Honda Prelude. The Honda did not have air-conditioning, but my friend who sold it to us assured me we wouldn't need it because the car had a moonroof that would let in all the refreshing air we could ever want. I chose to believe this.

The little red Honda was our primary vehicle for the next ten years, during which time our family doubled in number. Our first daughter was born on the hottest day of July in 1983, and my wife was in full-blown labor when I drove her to the hospital in a cramped little car with no air-conditioning. She was not reluctant to remind me of this fact between contractions. A moonroof may sound romantic at the point of sale, but it doesn't much impress a woman who finds herself pushing out a baby in ninety-nine-degree temperatures in a confined space. I was there.

Felicia Ford would eventually burst into flames beside a gas pump (never a good thing), and Betsy Buick just faded away. There were other lovable vehicles: the blue station wagon with woodgrain siding and drooping roof-liner that billowed up and floated down to rest upon my children's heads; and the burgundy minivan (also a woody) whose passenger window, not unlike Felicia's, was liable to retreat into the door for no apparent reason.

My wife and children love to tell stories about these four-wheeled members of our family. I love to hear them.

Motor on.

We Need a Little Christmas

Traditionally, the day after Thanksgiving is when we start decorating for Christmas at our house. I am presented with a choice: I can go with my wife to the mall on the National Day of Insanity, or I can stay home and help her decorate. No contest: Bring on the scuba-diving Santa ornament.

Decorating at our house is a major deal. Over the years, my wife has collected a tractor-trailer-load of Christmas decorations. We normally have four full-sized Christmas trees, each struggling under the weight of multitudinous ornaments and lights. When it comes to lights, my wife adheres to two guiding principles: one, they must be clear, not multicolored; and, two, there must be many of them—perhaps, and I'm not kidding, a couple of thousand lights per tree. We happen to enjoy a little tree with our lights.

Assembling and decorating four Christmas trees, each in accordance with its own theme, can take a few days. After the trees come the accessories: china settings for two tables, the snowman collection, the Santa collection, the little-ceramic-houses-with-snow-on-the-roof collection, and numerous candles, ribbons and shiny balls.

Her decorations are stored in two dozen Tupperware Rough Totes labeled in permanent marker. Over the span of twenty years and four moves, a few decorations have found their way to the wrong containers, which means we have to rummage through each one. Some containers hold decorations we no longer use, stuff we once considered tasteful but now wouldn't put on the doghouse.

When I've transported the decorations from the barn, up the steps and into the house and parked my hand trucks, I leave my wife to the particulars of removing lids and digging through her Yuletide pretties. I depart to do the Man's Work, which is to put up the outdoor lights.

After hanging Christmas wreaths on columns, doors and windows, I get down to the exciting part of my job, which is installing my custom-designed wiring and lighting system. Every wreath has its own dedicated spotlight, which makes for an angry mass of power strips and extension cords tangled up in the corner of my porch. It looks like a tumbleweed with a nasty attitude. This complex-but-elegant setup is my personal Christmas joy. The crowning jewel is the wireless remote I attach to the whole system so we can activate the lights from inside the house. At the push of a button, holiday guests hit the floor when their sympathetic nervous systems alert their brains that a 747 is landing on our front walk.

With our children grown, my wife is trying to talk herself into cutting back. She is thinking of putting up only one tree this year, the big one in the living room. That tree is home to hundreds of family ornaments we've collected over the years. When our children were babies, she began buying keepsake birthday ornaments each year. When they were older, the girls asked to pick out their own ornaments. Goodbye, Hallmark—hello, tacky. Amy chose a glowing pink flamingo, which set the bar for the rest of all time. Now, dangling from our family Christmas tree, beside the handcrafted angels and lambs our kids made in Sunday school, is a camouflage-clad Santa with a hunting rifle, Spider-Man perched on the side of a chimney, and a rainbow trout that looks so real I'm tempted to smear some tartar sauce on it. My wife hangs these interesting ornaments on the far side of the tree, but a motley group of elves conspires to make sure they always find their way to front and center.

Stop by for some eggnog. Attire is casual. Sunglasses are optional.

There Were Children in This House

There were children in this house. You can tell by what they left behind: Clothes and shoes. Trophies and crowns. Textbooks and yearbooks. Cell phones and video games. Report cards and refrigerator clippings. Hot curlers and nail polish. Snapshots and Disney videos.

Everywhere I go in this old house, I see the things they left behind. School awards are on display. A portrait of Katie in her bridal gown hangs on a wall at the base of the stairs. In the living room is a long bookshelf where until recently no fewer than thirty family photos were arranged just so, most of them of our children at different stages of life. Amy persuaded her mother to tone it down after we gave the room a fresh coat of paint and new curtains.

But for every visible reminder of the two girls who grew up here, there are hundreds of hidden reminders. While rummaging through a cabinet where my camera equipment was stored, I came across a poem Katie wrote when she was in high school. She titled it, "My Father's Love." It meant everything to me back then, but it meant even more to reread her words after she was grown and gone.

In a side pocket of a camera bag I found a batch of construction-paper vouchers Amy presented me on some long-ago Father's Day: "Good for one big hug." "Good for taking out one bowl of scraps." "Good for one hour of peace and quiet." "Never expires," promises the guarantee on the back of the book.

In the closet of Amy's old bedroom, there is a paper silhouette of her taped to the back wall. When I stacked my boxes there, I never even considered moving her picture. No matter how long we live here, the room will be hers, regardless of how much daddy-stuff I haul in to clutter it up.

The evidence of my children is everywhere, melded into the walls of the place. My daughters reside in every cranny, behind every door. I cannot go from one room to another without hearing them. They live here, even if they sleep someplace else.

That makes it hard for me to think about selling this house, even though I know it is too big for two people. It makes sense to think about downsizing. We moved here nine years ago when our oldest starting driving. We thought it would be a great place to raise teenagers—a house that was close to school, central to everything, and a big enough place for them to bring their friends. And we were right.

So when I think about leaving, I think about the fact that this is the last place our children lived with us. No future house will know that history. The next place will be our home, but it won't be theirs—it will just be Mom and Dad's house.

They still come—to watch a college football game and fill their bowls from Mom's Big Ol' Pot of Chili, or to watch cheerleading competitions on ESPN, or to touch base, to recenter. And when they back out of the driveway to go in separate directions toward their own lives, we stand at the back door and watch, our gratitude unspoken, unspeakable. We hold on, and we let go. As the taillights fade, I know there were children in this house. I can tell by what they left behind. It never expires.

Prince and Princesses

Animals have been collecting at our house for the past few years. It must be an unwritten rule: When children leave home, you replace them with pets. In our case, the pets are dogs and cats, although at various times in our family's history they were gerbils, hamsters, birds, frogs and hermit crabs.

Or fish. I've always been a dog man, but we had tropical fish back in the early days of our marriage, when we lived in an apartment. The fish couldn't fetch and never seemed particularly glad to see me. They also tended to go belly-up without warning. I was at work when my wife called with the news:

"Suckfish is dead."

"Wow."

"He's dead, and he's all bloated. What should I do?"

"Scoop him out with the little net."

"Ewww!"

We moved on to land critters. Over the next few years, our children had the usual pets (the aforementioned gerbils, hamsters, frogs and hermit crabs), and they had Millie, a devoted golden retriever who came to live with us when she was a puppy and was part of our family for fourteen years. For the rest of our daughters' lives, sweet Millie will be in their thoughts when they recall the days of tromping through the woods and riding their three-wheelers and Barbie Ferraris in the driveway.

Today, our children live elsewhere, but in their absence are two dogs and two cats. One of the dogs, Napoleon, has assumed the role of presumptive heir to our children's place in the pecking order. The remaining pets live outside—Napoleon reigns indoors—and are mere pretenders to the throne.

A mother doesn't stop being a mother after her children move away, and Napoleon is happy to play the part of the surrogate child. The attachment he feels to his momma is strong. Even though I feed the dog as often as my wife does, and despite the fact that I play with him in the floor and I'm the one to take him for a walk every day, Napoleon, if he's forced to choose, will pick me over her only if he believes I have a treat for him.

Food comes before his momma, but nothing else does. If my wife is on the couch watching television, Napoleon whimpers if she won't let him join her. If she reaches for the stack of throws we keep at the end of the couch, he goes nuts. He has learned that this is the most opportune time to persuade her to allow him on the couch. It's his cute little dance that does the trick—being "adorable," she calls it.

When my children were little, I often found myself wishing I could slow down their growing up. I'm a kid myself—I'd as soon join a game of kickball as golf—and I enjoyed playing with my girls. They're young women now, possessed of optimism and energy, embarking on exciting lives of their own making. They were at our house on Sunday with a husband and a boyfriend in tow, gathered around Mom's table for burgers and laughter. Katie sat by me. For a little while, the weight of adulthood vanished, and a grown woman turned into a little girl when her dad got silly and pretended to poke her in the ribs.

Banished temporarily to his room, Napoleon protested bitterly. The children had come home to reclaim their rightful throne.

Taking Cues from My Kid

Our youngest child will graduate from college in a few days. Seems only last week her mother was boohooing at the sight of her baby girl trying on her high school graduation gown.

It's incredible how the clock keeps getting faster. You stare at it and hope to stop it from moving, but you can't. It's like trying to stay awake during the late news to watch the weather report; you don't even realize your eyes have closed, and then you wake to the unsettling echo of your own snoring, and Jay Leno is ten minutes into his monologue.

When I was a boy, the yearlong countdown that began on December 26 represented an incomprehensible period of time. Now, instead of measuring my life in days, I lump my existence into chunks of years—decades, even. A mental game I play is to think of famous people and calculate how old I was when they were born. (For the first time in my life, it is possible that the next president of the United States will be younger than I am. Paradoxically, I find the thought both worrisome and comforting.)

This is the beginning of a midlife metamorphosis for me and millions of my fellow boomers. We're in a generational twilight zone,

one in which we're expected to remain productive members of society but also to start passing control of things to the next generation. It doesn't matter that we might not feel inclined to relinquish the control; the sad truth is that the remote will be gently lifted from our hands the moment we nod off during the late news.

It's actually reassuring to think someone younger is ready and willing to assume the responsibility for worrying about things. I've noted an acquiescence in some of my older friends, especially those who consider themselves "senior citizens." They don't worry as much. They live in the moment. They travel. They go out to eat. They don't fret too much about politics or elections. They seem to have readjusted their focus just in time for the third act.

My daughter is embarking on her post-student life in a time that feels scarier than when I graduated from college. The phrase "war on terror" wasn't part of my lexicon. A minimum-wage worker didn't have to work a full day to earn enough money for a tank of gas. There were more deep-blue-sky days, more snow days, and the seasons were more distinct.

I guess that's why I've tried to keep her in a bubble, to shield her from life's blunt edges as long as possible. The hardest thing about being a parent isn't in knowing how to protect her, but in recognizing when my protection starts to be a disabling thing, hindering her from learning how to protect herself. How much protection is too much? How little is too little?

Ultimately, the answer will come—but not from the sky, nor from a voice within me. The answer will come from my child. On a frigid January morning in 1986, she told her expectant mom she was ready to meet the world. I'm guessing she'll tell me, too.

Stop, Rest and Shop

Debbie and I recently spent a couple of nights at the charming High-lands Inn. It was just what the doctor ordered.

While my wife sampled the crisp mountain air in the form of a nap, I took the opportunity to learn some things about The High-lands (for some reason, I've always called it "The" Highlands) that I didn't know before. The town was founded about 1875 by two Kansas businessmen who, while studying a map, drew a line from Chicago to Savannah, then another from New York to New Orleans. The point of intersection that connected those four cities, they reasoned, would be a profitable place to build a town where busy travelers might stop, rest and shop.

Stop, rest and shop. Reminds me of the mnemonic device my children repeated after a firefighter visited their school: stop, drop and roll. Stop, rest and shop might not qualify as lifesaving advice, but it is certainly sanity-saving counsel. The best time for me to take a vacation is when I think I don't have time to take a vacation. When I'm most busy or overwhelmed, the worst thing I can do is plow ahead; I usually end up plowing in circles. Taking a break brings rest and a fresh perspective. It doesn't have to be two days at a quaint hotel in the mountains; it can be as simple as taking a walk around the block.

My wife took to heart the town fathers' invitation to stop, rest and shop. When we finally pulled the car into a parking lot after negotiating mountain passes with switchbacks severe enough to upend even the steadiest stomach, and after we completed a walking reconnaissance of the shopping district (all locked up for the evening), and after we enjoyed a supper of barbecue ribs served on a grocery sack that doubled as a place mat (it was a meal my wife believes was divinely ordained at the Creation), we rested.

Well, she rested. I read brochures. That's how I learned that The Highlands sits on a plateau 4,000 feet above sea level and receives ninety inches of rainfall annually, a fact I attempted to share with Sleepy-Grumpy when she rolled over and fluttered her eyelids in a flash of unconscious non-recognition. Had Sasquatch just loped in off the mountain and shimmied up the balcony, clutching a brochure and poking her in the shoulder, she would not have noticed the difference.

She did not recall my geography lesson the next morning, nor did she seem interested in learning more about the topography of the area when I asked if she wanted to go on a hike. "Hike?" she said, in much the same way someone might say the word, "Mildew?"

"Are there sidewalks along this 'hike'?" she asked. "Are there store windows displaying ridiculously expensive clothing and local handicraft? If so, then yes, I would love to go on this 'hike' of which you speak."

So we summoned up our strength and hiked all the way

downstairs and stuffed ourselves with eggs, grits, potatoes, bacon, toast, strawberry preserves, juice and coffee. The Flatlanders call this meal the Grand Slam. I shall henceforth call it the Sasquatch.

Then we went back upstairs and fell asleep. All in all, a pretty good vacation. The scenery was beautiful … in trifold, glossy four-color.

Turning the Ring

Our daughter graduated from college last week. After the ceremony, on the sun-drenched lawn of Clemson's Littlejohn Coliseum, after the first flurry of hugs but before the snapshots in front of the bronze tiger statue, she turned to me and said, "The saddest part was when I turned my ring around."

When a student becomes a graduate, it is tradition to reverse the direction of her university ring so that it faces outward. The turning signifies the wearer's transition from student to alumnus. It is a clear and unmistakable pivot, a shifting from one season of life toward another. It is a bittersweet moment: a celebration followed by the sound of a closing door.

Amy couldn't wait to graduate from high school. She was in a big hurry to get to the next chapter. When we accompanied her to freshman orientation four summers ago, the meetings in classrooms and meals in the dining hall stirred memories of my own college experience, prompting me to invoke fatherly prerogative and advise her to savor every single moment. I told her it would all go by much faster than she could ever imagine. On this point, she would come to agree with me.

When she was a student at Miss Lou's daycare, Amy was given the nickname "Aimless" by Mr. Dave, Miss Lou's husband. Amy would climb onto Mr. Dave's lap and play peekaboo, and Mr. Dave would refer to her as "Miss Aimless." The name stuck, and we used it a lot, particularly when she went through a gymnastics phase that lasted several years, rendering her physically incapable of crossing from one side of the room to the other without cutting a cartwheel or attempting a back-walkover. This spasmodic mode of locomotion often resulted in her slamming into walls or door facings. But even during the gymnastics years, she wasn't really aimless; she knew where she wanted to go, even if her way of getting there was occasionally off the beaten path.

Through her middle and high school years, her aim grew truer, and she accomplished most of the things she set out to do. But she sometimes had trouble sitting still while she studied. I grew accustomed to seeing her rehearse cheerleading moves in front of the mirror while her mother quizzed her for an upcoming test. Year after year, she set goals for herself and then checked them off, and I admired her for it. (I spent my formative years riding my bike and reading Archie comics.) She became an organized person in the same way that a honeybee is organized: What seems like random buzzing and darting is really controlled chaos leading to an elegant result.

The day after Amy's graduation, our family was back at Clemson, this time for a wedding. We had watched the bride and groom grow up alongside our kids. The outdoor wedding was a beautiful affair, with a lake and a pristine golf course serving as backdrop. The reception was held in an open pavilion, and the air thrummed with the energy of happy parents and friends, just as it had the previous afternoon at commencement. There was laughter and dancing, and Amy was there in the middle of it all, coaxing reluctant dancers into the circle of celebrants.

All eyes were on the revelers, and I saw again what I've seen a thousand times: Amy's ring of friendship, always pressing outward, extending to embrace everyone she meets.

Next Year

I don't know if it's old age or what, but on our recent family vacation I found myself unable to relax. For a whole year, I had looked forward to our trek to Garden City Beach, tasting the fried shrimp and hushpuppies and dreaming of wasting away afternoons under a beach umbrella with a good book. But when we finally got there, I couldn't enjoy the experience because the part of my brain that is preoccupied with the mundane stuff of home simply refused to let loose of it.

I'm sorry to whine. I blame my whining, like my worrying, on old age. Old age is a good excuse for all kinds of unflattering behavior, like getting all in a snit when we stopped for lunch on the way to the beach and the lady at the chicken place gave me two legs even though I explicitly requested a leg and a wing. "But I don't want two legs!" I fumed to my wife and daughter in a ploy for sympathy. Their response was to giggle. Giggle! My wife, in her patient mother/teacher voice, wondered if I would at least eat one chicken leg, since I had ordered that. I sulked and thought about resting firm on principle, but I decided a couple of chicken legs would carry me farther down the interstate than my righteous indignation. When my loved ones giggled, I tried to mask a half-smile, at which point the battle was lost. Better to eat not-chicken-wings under protest than to stage a hunger strike for a lost cause. In a parting gesture of defiance, I threw away half of my cole slaw. Yes, I did. A man has his pride.

But back to being on vacation and not being able to relax. I don't think I'm alone. Wave your beach towel if you, too, have had a hard time unwinding while on vacation. Okay, that's good. You can stop now. Seriously. People are looking.

It takes me almost the whole week at the beach to let go of the mental baggage that made the vacation necessary in the first place. By Thursday, I am beginning to embrace leisure, shifting to a lower gear. By then, however, it's almost time to leave, and I regret the days I wasted preoccupied with things of little importance. On the long drive home, I usually voice this thought: "Why is the ocean most beautiful on the day you leave?" I resolve that next year will be different. I will not pack work or worries in my suitcase ... next year.

I am not home twenty-four hours before pleasant memories of this year's vacation start to make themselves at home in comfy corners of my brain—like the afternoon my son-in-law and I walked to the pier and listened to an aging country-rock band with an earnest Linda Ronstadt look-alike belt out a hunka, hunka burning love. I also won't forget the expressions on my children's faces when they ordered a salad at a nice restaurant, and what emerged from the kitchen was a teeny wedge of lettuce with six morsels of bacon arranged around it like numbers on a clock—a pretty green-and-pork clock. At first we all pretended we had culture and this was a normal thing to eat, but then we broke form and started flinging insults at the teeny wedge of lettuce.

Next year, I'll leave my worries in the driveway.

Next year, we'll stay two weeks.

Next year.

Do Tell

It didn't take seeing Michael Phelps win eight gold medals to convince me I am not a kid anymore. No, regardless of the fact that I watched this young Olympian's conquest from the comfort of my easy chair, and despite the fact that I gained at least five pounds while watching the Olympics, snacking on sun-dried tomato-and-basil Wheat Thins and Breyers All-Natural Vanilla Ice Cream in all-out pursuit of my own gold medal in the Couch Potato All-Around, none of this is why I know I'm not young anymore. The reason I am finally sure—signed, sealed and certified by the IOC and waiting for my interview with Bob Costas—is because I forgot to shave half my face this morning.

Specifically, it was the bottom half I forgot to shave; anatomically, it was my neck. One minute, there I stood, gazing with practiced absence at the fifty-three-year-old hunk of glory in the mirror, scraping away the morning stubble with my Gillette Good News razor, when my thoughts drifted, as they tend to do, toward the coming fog that would be the detail of my day. The next minute, I'm rinsing my face and wondering why there's lather clogging up the sink.

Have you ever done something like that—something, well, just goofy—and even though nobody witnessed it, still you were embarrassed? Well, I was that guy—standing puzzled in front of the mirror, water and liquified Edge shaving gel puddling on the floor (where sat my dog, himself not exactly the poster boy for good sense, whose expression seemed to ask, what's wrong, dude?) and my first thought was: Should I keep this to myself?

I thought maybe I should, and for good reason: My wife likes to tell things she knows. My children understand that if they want to share some news with me, they shouldn't tell their mother first. Mom is plugged into a high-speed network that makes texting look like smoke signals. Her network is so quick, in fact, that I know what my children have told their mother even before they have finished telling her. It's her own special way of bending the space-time continuum.

So if I don't want others to know something, I don't tell her. For instance, I waited many years after we were married before I shared a physics conundrum that has stymied me since childhood. It goes something like this: If you place a board on the ground and stand on it, why can't you grab the edges of the board and lift yourself into the air? (Think about it. See what I mean?)

She really enjoyed telling that one. I should have kept my theory to myself. But I know this: If a thought is in my head, it's going to come out, which I understand is another sign of old age. So if I want to avoid being the punch line, I try to control the message by telling it first.

Which brings us back to where we started, with me admitting I forgot to shave half my face. Okay—there it is. Very funny. Now let's all just move along.

One more thing: I've learned from observation (and, lately, from personal experience) that as we age we're less hesitant to talk about things we once considered private. Next week: surgery scars.

Speechless

There are some things of sufficient impact to leave a fellow speechless. Seeing Hank Aaron hit his 715th home run was one; watching Neil Armstrong step onto the surface of the moon was another. Beyond such momentous events, there are others: watching your bride walk down the aisle toward you, witnessing the birth of your child, burying a parent, seeing your kid graduate from high school.

Oh—and here's another: watching a hairy-legged boy ask for permission to marry your daughter. That has happened to me twice.

The first time was a few years ago. We knew ahead of time why the boy was coming. We were ready. He was nervous. When he mustered the courage to ask the thing he'd come to ask, I said, "Why?" Judging from the sudden departure of color from his face, I thought the boy might throw up. But he gave a good answer, and I said, "Of course!" and we all made it through the ordeal without need of a cold wash cloth or a bucket.

The second time was last week. The boy, a former college baseball player, threw us a curve ball. When he called and asked if he could stop by on his way to play golf, we had barely five minutes to mobilize. "Why is he coming?" my wife asked. "I don't know," I said as casually as I could, even as my heart was speeding up. "Maybe he needs to borrow my clubs." Debbie said that didn't sound right. I didn't think so, either, but I pushed the thought away and tried to read my newspaper.

The boy arrived. The dog barked. I heard my wife greet him at the back door. I stayed in the bedroom, reading my newspaper—hiding. After a minute, Debbie opened the door and motioned for me to join them. I swallowed hard, folded the paper beside me, and shuffled in my sock-feet toward the kitchen like I was headed to the principal's office. I'd wanted nothing more than to come home to a quiet, uneventful evening. I don't do surprises well.

Before I had a chance to assess the situation, the boy looked me in the eye and came straight to it. He said he wanted to ask my daughter to marry him and hoped we would approve. I was at one of those crossroads you think about and wonder what you'll say when it comes (the last thing you think is that there'll be ink smudges on your fingers and nothing but socks on your feet) and all you can do is stand there while the mother of your child jumps up and down and squeals like a schoolgirl and you realize your mouth is open and no words are coming out and that unofficial permission has already been granted.

Finally, you feel the need to pose some sort of authoritative question, even if it is only a formality, and you start with something like, "Well, we think you're a fine young man ... " and your sweet little wife grinds her heel into your toe, which brings tears to your eyes, which makes the boy think you're getting emotional, bringing to an abrupt end any semblance of control you thought you had.

Our baby girl got engaged this week. If I was speechless when it happened, I'm not now. Being in this family just keeps getting better and better.

Field & Scream

We moved from town to country a couple of months ago. So far, I have stared down a charging woodland creature, dodged an unidentified object hurled at me from a moving car, and outrun a swarm of ill-tempered hornets.

All of these things happened while I was walking my dog, Gabbie, a part-beagle, part-border collie whose entire reason for living is the moment she sees me step out the back door and walk toward her pen. She literally jumps for joy.

And even though she's almost ten, she has lost neither the enthusiasm nor the energy she enjoyed as a puppy. She is all muscle (from all that jumping for joy, I suppose). It's all I can do to make her stand still long enough to snap on her leash. Then we're off, her nose to the ground, zigzagging and lurching ahead while I struggle to hang on.

As soon as we can, we get off the road and into a big open field that skirts the woods, where I unhitch Gabbie and let her run. And oh, how she runs! If a dog can know glee, Gabbie does. She bounds through the tall grass, stopping just long enough to sniff a paralyzed grasshopper, then she's off again, galloping toward the woods. Witnessing this euphoria is enough to make a bad day good.

I amble on across the field and leave her to chase the scents she finds in the woods. Before long, I know she will emerge, lift her nose to the breeze and sprint my way when she spies me in the distance. It's predictable.

Except when it's not. One evening she was thrashing around in the bushes at the edge of the woods. I thought she was coming toward me, so I waited near the spot where I thought my dog would appear, when a much larger creature, one with antlers and hooves, leapt forth and came straight at me. I would like to say my manly instincts sprang forth and I waved my arms and startled the buck into changing his course. I would like to say that. What I have to say, however, is that I flinched and let loose an involuntary girl sound that came out sounding like "Aiieee!!" Luckily, my squeak had the same effect as a full-throated "Haw!" from a seasoned cowpoke. The deer turned tail and bolted back into the woods, where Gabbie, if I know her (and I think I do), had her nose stuck down a chipmunk hole.

On another occasion, I thought I would do my Ralph Waldo Emerson impression and follow Gabbie into the woods, much to her delight. I walked behind her as she tried to inhale every molecule of dirt in her path. Problem was, there was a hornet's nest in the dirt in her path. She'd never encountered hornets before, so she had trouble connecting the dots between the buzzing about her ears and the brushfires erupting on her snout. For me, I figured it out pretty quick. When Gabbie saw me hotfooting my size-elevens out of there, she caught and passed me in two seconds. All that man's-best-friend stuff was ditched. It was every dog for herself.

Despite the perils of wood and field, I still find both preferable to walking along the road. People drive too fast in the country, and some of them throw things out the window—mostly bottles and cans, but also the occasional plastic baby bathtub. (I am not making this up.) My mailbox has been attacked twice, and, once, some teenage boys threw something at me as I walked my dog. They were laughing as they went past. I think I'll take my chances with Bambi and the bees.

You Might Be Getting Old

Over the life of this column I have used up a few barrels of ink visiting the same topics again and again. Most of what I have written fits predictably into one of the following categories: my wife and kids, my dogs, my childhood, all things NASA, general-purpose rambling, and the un-joy of aging.

In the early years I wrote about the delights of life with a young family. But now that I am eligible for membership in AARP (so far I have resisted their slick entreaties to join up), there are a growing number of columns that can be filed under the heading: "I'm Getting Old, And I Don't Like It."

As life slips by, we get caught in the drift of a subtle current and don't even know we're being carried along until one day we find ourselves cruising down the interstate, blissfully unaware that the turn signal has been blinking since our last stop, which was fifteen miles ago at the Cracker Barrel.

With a nod to Jeff Foxworthy, here are some signs that you (and I) might be getting old:

If you get antsy when you're not home before sundown, you might be getting old.

If you allow your annoying little dog to get away with behavior your children would never have attempted, you might be getting old.

If you turn down free tickets on the 50-yard-line because you'd rather curl up with a bowl of Breyer's vanilla ice cream and fall asleep watching the game on TV only to wake up with the upholstery fabric imprinted on your face, you might be getting old.

If you address the person waiting your table as "honey," you might be getting old.

If the person waiting your table addresses you as "honey," you might be getting old.

If you and your wife are coming home from a date and the sun gets in your eyes, you might be getting old.

If you have a nightlight in your bathroom but there are no children in your house, you might be getting old.

If you roll over and break your reading glasses because you fell asleep with them on top of your head, you might be getting old.

If you groan while either (1) getting on or (2) getting off the couch, you might be getting old.

If you get an itchy dialing finger when Bill Gaither shows up on TV with a new Homecoming video, you might be getting old.

If you know what it is to "dial" a phone, you might be getting old.

If you avoid candy apples and Sugar Daddys because of your expensive dental work, you might be getting old.

If you know the words to the "Gilligan's Island" theme song, you might be getting old. (Also: "The Brady Bunch," "The Addams Family.")

If it hurts your feelings a little when people make fun of Barry Manilow songs, you might be getting old.

If you hear the word "crown" and your first thought is not of the royal family, you might be getting old.

If it takes you less time to shower and shave than to type a text message on your phone, you might be getting old.

If your definition of date night is Mama Penn's and Walmart, you might be getting old.

If you forget what you were about to say, you ... dadgum ...

If you say "dadgum," you might be getting old.

Seasons

Fall is here. In the morning when I leave for work, a late-rising sun casts shafts of gold through the oaks in my neighbor's yard and into mine. Sunlight dances everywhere on a translucent coat of dew. The cats leave trails in the wet grass. The sky is so deep blue you can almost see the planets beyond. The earth seems to pause before rotating northward for the winter.

Later in the day, the quickening dusk beckons my future son-in-law and me outdoors to toss a football. On my evening walk, the dog keeps her nose to the ground, inhaling the odors left by a family of deer that bedded down in the tall grass the night before.

At midnight, when I take our other dog outside for the day's last opportunity for free-ranging, I stand still for several minutes and look straight up to see stars sparkling in a night sky that appears to have been squeegeed clean.

Fall: fresh, clear, renewing. I don't know if fall is my favorite season, but, for today, it is. Whatever season it happens to be at the moment—or, to be more precise, whatever season is in the process of becoming—is my favorite. As pleasant as summer is, with long days, beach vacations and Fourth-of-July cookouts with friends, when it starts to wind down I find myself looking forward to a change.

There has been a clarifying moment that signals this transition for me. For ten years we lived within walking distance of the high school in our town. On Friday nights I could hear the sounds of football—the public address announcer, the marching band, cheering fans—right there in my backyard. For me, that was the official start of fall, and I knew Halloween couldn't be far behind.

A few months ago we moved from our home in town to a house in the country, about three miles out. It is a nice place, smaller and newer. It was a smart move, since it will soon be just the two of us. Our last home was big and old and required a lot of work. But it was the perfect place for our family. Our children had their prom pictures made in the yard. They parked their first cars in the driveway. They opened their college acceptance letters at the little black mailbox beside the door. Our older daughter planned her wedding in that house. We had great neighbors. I jealously guarded my right to take an evening walk with the dog through the neighborhood. I am grateful for the years we had there, and I will always miss the old house. I literally still dream about the place.

But things change. Seasons pass—from winter, to spring, to summer ... and now, once again, to fall. And as a new season arrives, I know change has been good to me. Looking back over fifty-three years, it is clear that change, in all seasons, has been the engine that has powered my life and brought me to where I am today. I am a lucky man, with a good wife and happy children, and, as the song says, a house and a piece of land.

On a Friday night a few weeks ago, I went out to feed the dog. There, in my new backyard, I discovered to my private joy that I could still hear sounds coming from the high school football field—not as clearly as before, but there nonetheless. I was profoundly thankful for grace that eases the passage from one season to the next.

Dead Skunk in the Middle of the Dog's Mouth

With freedom comes responsibility. In exchange for letting my dog run free during our walk, I expected her not to attempt to swallow a live skunk. But she couldn't manage this one little thing, and now she is destined to spend the rest of her days on a leash. The skunk was less fortunate but did not go down without a fight.

It was a pleasant evening, late summer still, a pause in the seasons when sunsets linger on the horizon longer than seems physically possible. Since we'd moved to the country a few weeks earlier, I'd been taking walks with Gabbie through an open pasture and allowing her, for the first time in her ten years, to run free through the grass and nearby woods.

I've never seen a happier creature. When we walked up the road and jumped the ditch and made our way a hundred yards into the pasture, I would bend down and whisper, "Are you ready to run?" I gripped her collar and unhitched the lead, and Gabbie's legs twitched as she fought the urge to bolt.

"Are you ready?" I'd ask.

(Trembling.)

"Ready?"

(Whimpering.)

"GO!"

And she was gone, a black-and-white streak across the openness, stopping for a nanosecond to investigate the scent of a field mouse, then off again, zigzagging, circling, galloping away but always returning. Happy.

One evening Gabbie ran into the woods and spooked a buck, which crashed through the underbrush and nearly ran over me. It was an adventure I relished sharing with family and friends. With each retelling, the animal grew bigger and fiercer until it wasn't a deer at all, but a raging bull elk. And, in the retelling, I did not shriek like a little girl when the monster came at me; instead, with no regard for my own safety, I threw myself between the charging beast and my beloved pet. But I don't like to brag.

On another of our walks, Gabbie chased a chipmunk down a hole. Literally. She tried to follow the chipmunk down an opening that was the same diameter as her nose. Besides this and the incident with the angry antlered animal, the most exciting thing that happened during our walks was the time Gabbie sat down on a hornets' nest. The most exciting thing, that is, until: Monday Night Smack Down with a Skunk.

I'd just finished the pep talk. The dog was amped up. I released her, and she was off on a breakneck reconnaissance for chipmunks and deer droppings. I spied something hopping through the tall grass up ahead. A cat? No, cats don't hop. A rabbit? No, the wrong color—black and white, like a ...

The horror dawned on me just as Gabbie's radar locked on. Before I could intervene, the two animals had conjoined to form a horrible entity, a flailing nun's habit caught in a demon-possessed spin cycle. Gabbie had the skunk in her jaws, whipping it back and forth. I ran toward the calamity. The smell was vile. If you've ever smelled a skunk, multiply that by a hundred. Now spread it on a piece of bread and lay it on the back of your tongue. Now swim in it. Now try to run away from it.

Which is exactly what I did. That skunk was spewing out some putrefied high-octane stuff, and Gabbie was spreading the joy. I ran, but the skunk-on-toast taste on the back of my tongue ran with me. It stayed for days. I was physically ill. Now, even the faint odor of skunk brings on the queasies.

Yep, Green Acres is the place to be.

Christmas Tree Adventures

We're down to one Christmas tree at our house. There was a time in the not-too-distant past when a visitor could make a complete circumnavigation of our yard and never lose sight of at least one Christmas tree through the windows of our house. For several years we had four full-sized trees, laden with decorations, and there were several smaller tabletop trees scattered throughout the house.

Those multiple-tree years, in retrospect, were fun and made for lots of conversation, but I'm sure I've forgotten much of the work that went into getting them put up and decorated. Now that we're again a one-tree household, I am reminded of the very first artificial Christmas tree we bought.

It was 1983, and my wife and I, along with five-month-old Katie, found ourselves in the Christmas tree aisle at Walmart. "I won't have a plastic Christmas tree in my home," I said. "It just wouldn't be Christmas without a real tree!" With that pronouncement, I wheeled the shopping buggy around and sped away from the fake Christmas tree department. "However," I said, slowing, "it was on sale."

Minutes later, I was in the parking lot, stuffing the branches, trunk and pedestal of a plastic Christmas tree into the back seat of our tiny two-door Honda because the box would not fit. All the while, I was pounded by the worst rainstorm since the Great Flood. My wife, who was snug inside the car, kept asking if there was anything she could do to help. She told me later that every time I dove into the box to gather an armload of imitation pine needles, she collapsed in a heap. Each time I reemerged from the box, dripping, she stifled her hysteria long enough to gaze at me through her tears (I thought it was rain) and ask, "Honey, is there anything I can do to help?"

"No, I'll be through in a second!" I said in my reassuring hunter-gatherer voice, diving back into the box, her giggles trailing behind.

Obtaining a Christmas tree, especially a retail one, should not be this hard. I remember Christmases past when my dad would call to my brothers and me: "Come on—let's go see what we can find!" When I heard that, I would sneak into the kitchen and steal my mom's favorite kitchen knife so we could go … Christmas tree hacking!

Christmas tree hacking is an experience all sons and fathers should share. You pile into your dad's pickup truck with your brothers and bounce down the road toward the open country, eyes riveted on the horizon, looking for the perfect Christmas tree. Once you spot The Tree, you pull over and wait until there are no other cars coming. Then you and your brothers run over to the tree and begin hacking it with the knife. Anyone who has ever attempted to fell a cedar with a kitchen knife knows that these trees have built-in defenses. The bark has goo that makes the knife stick to the trunk every time you take a swing at it. Having one of these trees in your living room at Christmas was both a family affair and a real accomplishment.

I once declared that a plastic Christmas tree would never spread its branches in my home. Things have a way of changing. That's okay. What matters is not the kind of tree you have, but who you're sitting with while you admire it.

Mr. Third Verse

When I was nineteen, I was asked to lead hymns at my church on Sunday nights. I'd never led a hymn in my life, and I didn't know the difference between a bass clef and a baseball, but I said yes. It was the adventure, I suppose, but I also enjoyed the attention. Vanity has a way of working its way into even the most noble of aspirations.

I'd been on the job a few months, and my conducting skills had advanced to only slightly better than robotic. (I practiced my conducting in the mirror; I thought the congregation actually paid attention to that sort of thing and couldn't sing a hymn if I waved my arms in the wrong time signature. I soon learned that the congregation rarely looks at the song leader, and they take their cues from the pianist and organist, the real song leaders.)

A lady in my church, Mrs. Reba Wansley, wrote a story about me and published it in the newspaper, complete with a photo of a smiling teenager balancing a hymnal in one hand and waving the other hand in a knowledgeable manner while pretending to hold forth on Love Lifted Me. I don't remember much about the story, except that, near the end, she summarized my virtues with this observation: "And he never leaves out poor old Mr. Third Verse."

To this day, more than thirty years later, I still think about the late Mrs. Reba Wansley with affection and a twinge of guilt whenever I leave out Mr. Third Verse, which I rarely do. The congregation at Tabernacle Baptist Church in Pelzer can thank Mrs. Reba for the hundreds of third verses we sang over the last twenty-six years while the Sunday roast was overcooking.

To give Mrs. Reba her due, however, there are some things you might miss if you leave out the third verse. For instance, you might never know that "His heart is touched with your grief and despair" (Have Faith in God) or that God's bountiful care "sweetly distills in the dew and the rain" (O Worship the King) or that "sickness and sorrow, pain and death are felt and feared no more" (On Jordan's Stormy Banks). I could go on; we could have an all-day singing.

I will soon be retiring as Tabernacle's song leader after having the privilege of serving the sweet and generous people there since 1982. Tabernacle is the second-longest thing I've ever done—longer than I've been a parent, longer than any job I ever held, longer than I lived with my parents. The only thing I've been a part of that's longer is my marriage, and that by only a few months. I will be worshipping with my wife, the pianist (and, hence, the real song leader) at Earle Street Baptist Church in Greenville. I plan to make the transition from someone who leads songs to someone who sings while blissfully ignoring the song leader.

If many hymns have four verses, I am now singing the third verse of my life's song. I don't know how far into the verse I am—maybe just beginning, maybe closer to the middle, maybe later—but I know there are melodies yet to be found. I look forward to uncovering them. While there are some sweet songs one might naturally expect to find (having more time with my wife, playing with grandchildren), I imagine there are others that will come unexpected, as grace from above.

Thank you, Mrs. Reba. Thank you, Tabernacle. I'm feasting on the riches of His grace (third verse, He Keeps Me Singing).

Catching Up

My dad died many years ago, but I sometimes still dream about him, and in my dreams he is alive. I don't realize he is supposed to be gone, and his presence with me feels natural. When I wake up, my chest aches with the dawning realization, yet again, that it was only a dream. What comes next is profound gratitude for the gift of a dream, then a sort of warm afterglow.

Short-term memory has never been an asset of mine. When I'm sure I won't forget something, I usually do; I lose the memory, even though I try hard to recall the thing I was so sure I wouldn't forget. Sometimes I keep a pad and pen by my bed in case I think of something in the middle of the night, although I am usually too sleepy to get up and write it down.

But with this dream, I did write it down. I dreamed I was in a room playing a guitar when my dad walked in. "Have you seen my new guitar?" I asked my father, the man who taught me how to play. He held it up and examined it, his eyes scanning the fretboard and lingering on the tuning pegs. Then he set it on his lap and began to play. There was a soothing predictability to his picking; I knew his stylings by heart. His fingers danced across the strings, and I knew where they were going, like knowing the words to a song I'd sung a hundred times.

Then, as dreams sometimes go, he and I were walking along a street in my neighborhood, a place he didn't live to see. It suddenly occurred to me that I should have told someone where we were going, but then I remembered with relief that I was with my dad, which meant I didn't have to worry about anything at all.

We walked without saying much. I kicked some acorns to see how far they would bounce down the street. "I wish I had practiced more," I said.

"Me, too," said my dad, the man who practiced every day.

More walking, more quiet, then me again: "I wish I had studied harder in school." I tossed a stick into the woods.

"Yep," my dad said. "You never really catch up."

And then I woke up, and the dream was over, except for the fading echo of my father saying, "You never really catch up."

Who doesn't have regrets? I squandered opportunities when I was young. I didn't practice much, and I didn't study hard. In college, I didn't take advantage of all that was available for the taking. I enjoyed life, and I did little more than my classes demanded. I preferred spending a spring afternoon tossing a Frisbee to being holed up in the library with a textbook. On those occasions when I was compelled to spend several hours studying (that is, when a paper was due or a final exam was staring me in the face), I found the work rewarding, and I determined to apply myself more faithfully. Then would come the peripheral flash of a Frisbee, and I was off again. Full of good intentions, I thought there would always be more time.

It's not uncommon to look back over one's life and linger too long on the regrets. We've all done it. But this is not about that. This is about a son hearing an understanding word from his dad and knowing all will be okay.

The Best Job I Ever Had

The best job I ever had wasn't the one that paid the most or had the best benefits package. It wasn't in the tallest building in the middle of a big-city business district.

The best job I ever had included such duties as sweeping the floor, taking out the trash and making deliveries. It included night work. It involved handling chemicals that turned my fingertips yellow. It required that I punch a time clock.

The best job I ever had was one I coveted from the moment I first imagined it. I was a newlywed, visiting at my wife's parents' house, browsing through their copy of the Belton News. I scanned the small town news, the folksy reports by rural correspondents, the birth announcements and a personal column written by the associate editor, and I thought: I can do that.

A few weeks later, when I heard that the Belton News had a job opening, I called the publisher, Joe Coward. He met with me and we got along well, but he'd already offered the job to someone else. I thought the door to my journalism career was closed.

A few days later, the telephone in our apartment rang. It was Bill Meade, publisher of The Journal in Williamston, South Carolina. Joe Coward had told him about me, and he wondered if I would be interested in talking with him about a job at his newspaper.

I met with Mr. Meade at his office the next evening. After reviewing my background, he asked me to name my two state senators, which I managed to do. He asked me who my congressman was, and I knew that, too. Then he asked me who my county councilman was. I had no idea. He asked me which had the larger operating budget: the county government or the local school district. Again, I was stumped.

He said that if I wanted to work for him, I would have to know all that and more. I asked for a chance to prove myself. He assigned me to cover an American Legion baseball game. Then he told me to find an engaging person in the community and write a human-interest story. After I completed those assignments, he offered me a job. I couldn't believe my good fortune.

For the next two years, I looked forward to going to work every day. I learned how to write concise news copy. I learned how to take photos and develop them, how to interview tight-lipped high school football coaches, how to decipher police reports. I learned how to use a wide-angle lens to photograph a prize-winning watermelon so that it looked even more impressive than in real life.

I also learned that old men would loiter on the sidewalk outside the pressroom around lunchtime on Wednesday and wait for the first newspapers to roll off the press. People would be waiting for their copy of the Journal when I delivered stacks of papers to country stores later that afternoon. I learned that our newspaper mattered to people. I learned there was satisfaction to be found in the weekly cadence of what we did.

Today, when I walk into a place that smells of printer's ink, it is 1982 again, and I am in the pressroom with my coworkers enjoying a midmorning break with a bottle of Coca-Cola and a pack of Lance crackers.

When I left The Journal, Bill Meade shook my hand and wished me well, and he told me I would never find another job more fulfilling.

He was right. I often miss the best job I ever had.

Change

My wife will tell you I don't do well with change. I like the status quo.
If you tell me the grass is greener on the other side, I will say that my
grass is green enough, thank you. I crave stability. Adventure is for
Batman.

My car is sixteen years old and has 205,000 miles on it. I could
drive it another 100,000 miles and never complain. My wife's minivan is twelve years old and has 220,000 miles on it, and the paint is
peeling off the hood. For me, her car is just getting broken in. For
her, it is just broken.

I have had the same job for ten years, and it felt like I was job-hop-
ping when I left my previous employment after fourteen years. Until
recently, I had a pair of yard shoes that I purchased when I was in
college more than a quarter-century ago. When I threw them out, it
felt wasteful.

For someone who likes his change at a glacial pace, the past few
years have been a real challenge to my tranquility. Both my children have graduated from college. The older one got married, and
the younger is planning a wedding for next summer. In the last few
months, we have sold our home of ten years and bought a house in
a brand new place. I have had to adjust to a new lawn mower after
riding my reliable old Snapper for twenty years. The Snapper was a
booger to start, but I knew how, and there was a reassuring predictability to the process.

At my church, where I have stood behind the same lectern and led the great old hymns for more than twenty-six years, I have seen children be born, grow up, marry and have children of their own. Our nursery department should have a revolving door. Just when toddlers get to the point where they're not afraid of me, they grow indifferent to me.

Change happens. Keep it moving, buddy. Out of the way. People have places to be. Nothing to see here.

Except there is something to see. Even when our children are asleep, they are breathing and evolving. When we look away, even for a moment, we miss something.

At the side entrance to our church, there is a small aluminum overhang, a covered area where people drive up to drop off or pick up passengers when it's raining. The children like to gather there and climb the metal poles that support the overhang. Of all the places in our church where one might expect to find children—the nursery, the gym, the front steps—you're just as likely to find them there, taking turns shinnying up the pole to touch the awning above. It may be years before they're strong enough to reach the top, but they won't stop trying. It's a rite of passage.

Last Sunday morning I looked out the window, thinking about something else, and I almost didn't notice the cluster of children gathered around the old steel pole, its black paint rubbed thin by generations of hopeful climbers. But I did notice, and I remembered my own children, climbers themselves, and I offered a prayer of thanksgiving for the change they have brought to my life.

Afterword

We left off with Debbie and me moving to the country and our daughters getting married and starting families of their own. A lot has happened in the years since.

Katie and Josh live nearby and have two sons, Jake, four, and Graham, seven months old. Those boys are the sons I never had. Jake enjoys exploring the woods and fields with me, and Graham beams when I talk to him. I relish the moments I have with them, and I am filled with warmth when I think about watching them grow up and become the young men they are destined to be.

Amy and Ryan live a couple of hours away and have given us a granddaughter, Miller, who is a year and a half old. Miller looks like her dad and acts just like her mother. We recently had the opportunity to keep her for a few days while her parents were out of the country. When I rocked Miller to sleep at night, and as Debbie and I synced ourselves with her routines, I was transported back to the fleeting days of my daughters' childhoods. I had no idea the years would pass so quickly. I am grateful for the gift of grandchildren so that I can live those days again.

Debbie's mom passed away a few months ago, and her leaving has left a deep and empty hole in our lives. The loss is most acute for her husband and daughters, of course, but her steady presence in all our lives is only now being fully appreciated.

Gabbie, the hyperbolic beagle-border collie, died last year and is buried in our backyard. Napoleon, the little yappy house dog, has a cataract in one eye but otherwise is healthy and reigns supreme in our living room. Yard cats Puddin' and Ty-Bird have been joined by a walk-up stray we dubbed Edna. Our backyard neighbors have a pot-bellied pig named Wilbur.

Debbie continues to teach music in an elementary school and says she enjoys it more as the years go by. Her piano playing still hypnotizes me. She keeps up with everybody on Facebook and shares the pertinent details with me. We have settled into a comfortable rhythm of work, church and quiet evenings at home. She still likes to feel safe.

As for me, I enjoy taking walks around the neighborhood at sundown and watching the planets come out. It's a time when I recenter my thoughts on the things that matter most, which are the things that have always mattered most: my wife and girls and their husbands, and now our grandchildren—all at the center of my universe.

November 2014

CPSIA information can be obtained at www.ICGtesting.com
Printed in the USA
LVOW08*0603130115

422428LV00001BA/2/P